john wycliffe

The Dawn of the Reformation

John Wycliffe

John Wycliffe

The Dawn of the Reformation

by David Fountain

MAYFLOWER CHRISTIAN BOOKS

The Publishing Branch of
MAYFLOWER CHRISTIAN BOOKSHOPS CHARITABLE TRUST
114, Spring Road, Sholing. Southampton. Hants.

ISBN 0 907821 02 2

Typeset by Print Co-ordination   Macclesfield   Cheshire   England
Printed in Finland by K.J. Gummerus Osakeyhtiö, Jyväskylä

To the members of Spring Road Evangelical Church for their enthusiastic support in the production of this book. Some have been very closely involved in the typing, graphics, assisting with material, reading of the copy and in its publication. I have been grateful for their advice, encouragement and, above all, prayer, because we are still involved in the same spiritual warfare that took place 600 years ago.

About the Author

David Fountain was educated at Dulwich College and studied history at St. Peter's Hall, Oxford, where he obtained his M.A. He has been pastor of Spring Road Evangelical Church, Sholing, Southampton, since 1955. He has written a number of books on historical themes including:-
1970: The Mayflower Pilgrims and their Pastor (350th Anniversary)
1974: Isaac Watts Remembered (300th Anniversary of his birth)

Other Mayflower publications include:
A Stone Made Smooth
         – Autobiography of Wong Ming-Dao
Spiritual Food
         – Selected Writings of Wong Ming-Dao
A Light Shines in Poland

List of Contents

Illustrations

Colour Plates

Canterbury Pilgrims

Uproar in St Paul's showing Chaucer, Wycliffe, John of Gaunt, the Bishop of London, the Archbishop of Canterbury and the Earl Marshal.

Illustrations on pages 4, 67, 107, 125 and Time Chart by R. M. Goodridge.

Acknowledgements

The cover, 'The Dawn of the Reformation',
by W.F. Yeames, by kind permission of the
Suter Gallery, Nelson, New Zealand.
'Canterbury Pilgrims', by Kenneth Riley, by
kind permission of the National Geographical
Society.
Wycliffe's Bible by kind permission of the
Dean and Chapter of Hereford Cathedral.
S.M. Houghton of Abingdon for his
collection of illustrations.
The Evangelical Library, Chiltern St.,
London., for source material.

I would like to thank Jean Chenery for her
work in typing the manuscript, and Andrew
and Anne Fountain for editing the book and
planning the lay-out.

Foreword

I am very pleased to write a foreword to David Fountain's book on John Wycliffe, for we owe him a debt of gratitude for writing such an excellent account of that great Reformer's life and teaching in such a readable manner, and all within the compass of the understanding of the average person who may wish to know about these important matters.

The contribution that John Wycliffe made to the Reformation in England and to the special character of English Protestantism was immense, and the author brings this out in the most effective and helpful way. Wycliffe has not received as much attention as the other later Reformers, yet in some respects it can be argued that he was the greatest of them all. He has been termed 'the morning star' of the Reformation, which is a beautiful description of him, but he can with greater justice be called 'the rising sun' of the Reformation, for what he had to teach was integral to that great movement of the sixteenth century.

That, however, gives rise to a question in my mind: Is the sun which rose upon our nation with Wycliffe now setting? When we consider the widespread ignorance which now prevails regarding the Bible and the general trend in the Protestant churches to neglect their doctrines and their heritage, it may seem so, and there are those who undoubtedly welcome the fading of the light. But that is all the more reason for us to seek to revive interest in this great man and to make more widely known the truth about him and the blessings to our nation which resulted from his life and work.

This book will, I am sure, contribute in a large measure to this and will encourage us to remember these important things: First, that the truth of God is the same. The message of salvation that Wycliffe discovered in Scripture is the same as that which the Reformers later discovered, and which has been held by Bible-men throughout the ages. We must ourselves be gripped and held by that truth today, in an age that is credulous, restless and conditioned by change. Secondly, the opposition of the world is the same. An outstanding trait of Wycliffe's character was obedience to God's Word. He went on faithfully whether men were with him or not. We would do well also to place no trust in the fickle allegiance of men, but to continue in obedience and fidelity to the truth which God has revealed to us in his Word. Thirdly, the errors that arise in the church are the same. They keep recurring with astonishing regularity, yet always appear new and excitiing to those who are led astray by them. The popular religion of Wycliffe's day and the willingness of church leaders to pander to it are not so very different from our own time.

This book will do much to strengthen the cause of true religion and preserve among us the light that began to shine again upon our nation with that great man of God, John Wycliffe, over 600 years ago.

David N. Samuel.

Author's Preface

I cannot recall exactly when I first became interested in John Wycliffe, but it must have been before I went to Oxford to read history. The late Professor K.B. MacFarlane, fellow of Merton College (an authority on Wycliffe), was giving a series of lectures on Wycliffe and the Lollards. Such was my interest, even before hearing him, that I attended these, although they were not on my course. I still have the lecture notes, written thirty years ago!

Since that time I have collected quite a number of volumes on the subject. I was especially pleased to obtain Vaughan's two volumes on the life of Wycliffe, as they are almost unobtainable and extremely useful.

In 1968 I was asked to deliver a lecture on Wycliffe at the Conference of "Puritan and Reformed Studies" at Westminster Chapel. This gave me an opportunity to go into the subject in depth, and visit the British Museum. Since then I have collected more material, and have been waiting for the 600th anniversary of his death. There have been very many books written about him, though most of them during the nineteenth or early twentieth century. I have sought to glean from them what I felt was of most value and interest. I have not gone into the many different ways of spelling his name, or which of the many paintings of him is most likely to be accurate. Neither have I dealt with social events of his day that strictly speaking have no bearing on the theme. A bibliography of those books that I have found most helpful appears at the end of the book.

There are many things that could be said about a man who has had more biographies written of him than any other medieval person. As pastor of a local church I have endeavoured to deal with matters that are not only interesting and edifying, but of particular relevance today. It has not been an easy task to avoid the danger of being too academic and boring the reader, or being too popular and losing credibility. I have quoted a great deal from Wycliffe because he speaks so well for himself, and from others because some of my assertions may take the reader by surprise and I have felt the need for the support of those whose scholarship is beyond question.

John Wycliffe was truly a great man by any standard. God has given England few such men. I trust the reader will come to the same conclusion and be profoundly grateful for this man.

David Fountain

Note: the words of John Wycliffe, except for his sermons in chapter 12, are set in a different type face.

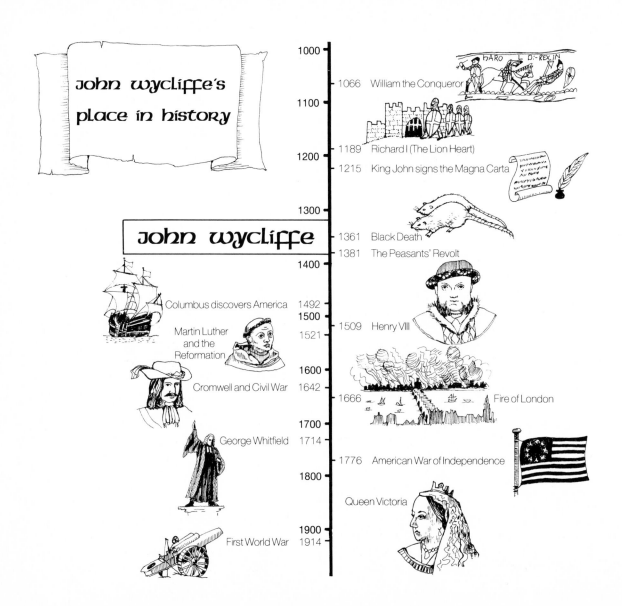

John Wycliffe's place in history

1000		
1066	William the Conqueror
1100	
1189	Richard I (The Lion Heart)
1200	
1215	King John signs the Magna Carta
1300	

John Wycliffe

1361 Black Death
1381 The Peasants' Revolt
1400

Columbus discovers America — 1492
1500
Martin Luther and the Reformation — 1521
1509 Henry VIII
1600
Cromwell and Civil War — 1642
1666 Fire of London
1700
George Whitfield — 1714
1776 American War of Independence
1800
Queen Victoria
1900
First World War — 1914

1.

Growing up in the Dark.

In a little village in the West Riding of Yorkshire, about 660 years ago, a child was born. He was to change the course of English history perhaps more than any other single person. He was born at a time when spiritual darkness lay across almost the whole of Europe.

But soon the dawn would break. God had prepared a champion against the forces of darkness. Probably the most brilliant man of his time, he was illuminated and governed by the Word of God. He and his followers had such a profound effect on the spiritual life of this land that 200 years later, at the height of the Reformation, John Fox was able to say in his famous 'Book of Martyrs', "Certainly, the fervent zeal of those christian days seemed much superior to these our days and times."

Early Life

There is considerable uncertainty about the date of John Wycliffe's birth, but it is generally considered to be about 1324. We know very little about his family background, and little indeed of a personal nature about the man himself. What we do know of him comes through his writings. We see here a man of clear understanding, vast knowledge and strong conviction.

It is known, however, that he was born in Yorkshire, six miles from Richmond, in a village that is still called 'Wycliffe'. This is the only place in England that has ever had that name. His surname may have been taken from his birthplace, as was often the case, rather than coming from his parents. From

The church at Wycliffe

the Conquest in 1066 to the year 1606 this village was the residence of the family with the name of 'Wycliffe', who were lords of the manor of Wycliffe and patrons of its rectory. John of Gaunt was the feudal overlord of that part of the country, and it is likely that there was some connection between this fact and the fact that, later, he became Wycliffe's patron. Doubtless, his academic skill was recognised early because there were many schools throughout the land, and he went up to Oxford in due course to 'enter the Church'.

Changes in Society

Wycliffe was born at a very important time in church history. England was emerging from the Middle Ages as a distinctive nation. The English language was coming into general use and was widely understood. Oxford University at this period had come to surpass Paris, and was the leading University in Western Europe. There was great emphasis on academic qualifications. Wycliffe was to gain great respect throughout the country because of his tremendous learning, for learning was held in very high esteem. The Church was ruled by an aristocracy of university graduates, and these men were considered useful to the State. Many bishops were no more than Civil Servants, and often Royal servants were rewarded by being made bishops. Few men rose to the top through any Church or any Royal service without a degree. Wycliffe was born into a society where academic attainment was more important than anything else, and having such a wonderful mind, it was in the providence of God that he would be able to use it to such good effect.

Medieval Darkness

He grew up at a time when the influence of the Papacy was at its height. Life for the peasant of Wycliffe's day has been described graphically:

. . . he stood or knelt on the floor of the church each Sunday, [he] could not follow the Latin words, but . . . watched what he revered and heard the familiar yet still mysterious sounds. Around him blazed on the walls frescoes of scenes from the scriptures and the lives of saints; and over the rood-loft was the Last Judgment depicted in lively colours, paradise opening to receive the just, and on the other side flaming hell with devil executioners tormenting naked souls. Fear of hell was a most potent force, pitilessly exploited by all preachers and confessors, both to enrich the Church and to call sinners to repentance." (Trevelyan).

The peasant could not expect any preaching from the resident priest, but he would get it from the preaching friar, and from the travelling pardoner, with his wallet "bret full of pardons, come from Rome all hot". Besides these religious roundsmen there were others who would travel through the winding, muddy roads and green lanes of England: minstrels, tumblers, jugglers, beggars and charlatans of every kind, living off the poor peasants. The peasant knew something of the sayings of Christ and Bible stories, but they were so embellished by the friar's sensational and entertaining sermons that he would not know truth from error. He never saw a Bible in English, and if he could have seen one he would not have been able to read it.

The Power of the Church

The most disturbing feature about the life of the peasant, and the message that he was used to hearing, was that he was in bondage to the Church and its sacraments. Pardon for sin depended on the particular acts of the peasant. These were corporal penance, pilgrimage, besides the gift of money which could relieve him from penance, and the payment for special Masses for the dead. 'Penance' was at this time being replaced by 'payment'. The exploitation of sin and the guilty conscience was the most terrifying and corrupting aspect of the relationship between the priest and the poor peasant in Wycliffe's day. In the hawking of pardons the Church reached its lowest depth, and it was not only

The Friar (Canterbury Tales)

Wycliffe who attacked such corruption, but others before him and after. The best known was Chaucer, the worldly-wise man. In his story of the pilgrims who journeyed to Canterbury he describes the unprintable reply of 'Mine Host' to the Pardoner when he tries to sell him his wares. Chaucer, who was a friend of Wycliffe's and thought highly of him while not agreeing with his theological opinions, supplies a very clear picture of just how bad things were in Wycliffe's day. His 'Canterbury Tales' are known to many people today. The pilgrims included a number of disreputable clerics. In view of the fact that Wycliffe spent much of his time attacking the friars, Chaucer's description of the friar is of particular interest.

Ful swetely herde he confessioun
And pleasant was his absolucioun
He was an esy man to yeve penaunce
Then as he wiste to have a good pitaunce
For unto a poure order for to yive
Is signe that a man is wel y-shrive
   [absolved]
For if he yat, he dost make avaunt
   [boast]
He wiste that a man was repentaunt
For many a man so hard is of his herte
He may not wepe although hym sore
   smarte
Therfore in stede of wepyinge and
   preyers
Men moote yive silver to poure freres.

In other words the friar was willing to accept money instead of tears as a sign of repentance. The local priest found that the friar heard his confessions for him on easier terms!

The neediest of the people were neglected by these men, and Chaucer continues:

He knew the Taverners wel in every
   town
And every hostiler and tappestere
   [barmaid]
Bet than a lazar [leper] or beggester
   [beggarwoman].

The friars had started well in the days of Francis of Assisi, and to begin with, even Wycliffe thought highly of them. But the four

Geoffrey Chaucer

Orders – Franciscans, Dominicans, Carmelites and Augustinians – had become corrupt and Wycliffe was to spend much of his energy exposing them, and then replacing them with his 'Bible-Men'.

Originally the friars were "men preaching Christ with burning love and conviction", but had degenerated, and responded to "the love for novelty". The friar-preacher "spread truth and confusion about the ancients indiscriminately, in such a way as to give pleasure" (Workman). The medieval sermon gave equal reverence for the Vulgate (the Latin Bible) and for the Fathers of the Church. No point was held to be proven until supported by both. Sermons were not expositions of Scripture, but stories in which Scripture, traditions and fables were all mixed up. In the mind of laymen there could be little distinction between Bible stories and other matter. A literature of this sort existed in the common language both in prose and verse. In short the people were confused and exploited.

The Civil Service

The common people were under the influence not only of the parish priest and the friar, but also the Civil Service that was virtually controlled by the clergy. It monopolised all secretarial work and the principal offices of state. The influence of the Church reached a point where the clergy almost seized power. This happened in Italy, Spain and, to some degree France, when at a later date political life and the liberty of the individual was crushed. The very struggle of the secular powers to rid themselves of the domination of the Church draws attention to its tremendous power. The clergy possessed more than half of the landed property of the kingdom. If a man died without leaving anything to the church they took over his affairs.

The Papacy

The Papacy itself had sunk to its lowest depth. In the fourteenth century the Pope was described as 'Our Lord God the Pope'. The removal of the Papacy from Rome to Avignon in France, had a profound effect on the attitude of Britain because we were continually at war with the French. The enormous sums of money that went to the Vatican through direct taxation, and the assumed right to dispose of the offices of the Church were especially irritating, particularly when there was a suspicion that the money helped to pay for the armies of our enemies.

In Fox's description of the early days of Wycliffe, we can see the darkness in which he was brought up at Oxford. "There was no mention nor almost any word spoken of Scripture. Instead of Peter and Paul men occupied their time in studying Aquinas and Scotus. Scarcely any other thing was seen in the churches, or taught or spoken of in sermons . . . but only heaping up of certain shadowed ceremonies upon ceremonies. The people were taught to worship no other thing but that which they did see, and they did see

**Balliol College, Oxford,
at the time of Wycliffe**

almost nothing which they did not worship."
It is not surprising that the appearance of the
Black Death when Wycliffe was a young man,
was regarded as a terrible visitation from on
high.

Oxford

The University was very different in
Wycliffe's day from now. In 1360 there were
only six colleges with less than 75 members,
but these were mostly graduates. MacFarlane
tells us that there were some 1,500
undergraduates, mostly clerks of the Church.
Their studies were most exacting. An
undergraduate starting at 15 would be at least
33 before he had completed his training. One
third of the starters would become Bachelors
and one sixth Masters. All examinations were
oral because of the great stress laid on
disputation and debate – in which Wycliffe
excelled! He was forty before he finished,
having allowed his studies to be interrupted
by administrative and other duties. Although
he obtained his B.A. in 1356, he did not take
his Doctor of Divinity until 1372. The
schoolmen set great store by disputation:
"This exercise is far more useful than reading
since by it doubts are resolved. Nothing is
perfectly known which has not been
masticated by the teeth of disputation. Minds
thus sharpened could not but be enquiring."
This speculative licence permitted in the
'Schools' accounts for the fact that it was only
when Wycliffe's teaching appeared to subvert
the whole University that the authorities
brought themselves to decisive action against
it.

Merton, the college at which Wycliffe spent
some years, was distinguished by two of its
scholars, William Occam and Duns Scotus,
who had been unequalled in their time.
Bradwardine was also one of its professors
who was finishing his career at about the same
time that the young Wycliffe was starting his.
He was among the first mathematicians and
astronomers, but was more attracted by the
Word of God, and came to receive the
doctrines of Sovereign Grace. Most of his
contemporaries, true medieval schoolmen,
searched into the essence of things to explain
all mysteries, but Bradwardine was ready to
accept what God had revealed in his Word.
He was rewarded, and saw the path which
others missed. He taught the simplicity of the
Gospel, rejecting 'Pelagianism' which taught
men to trust in religious activity and the power
of their own will for salvation. He told his
hearers that salvation could come only from
the sovereign grace of God. Bradwardine was
a great philosopher, but a greater theologian.
His fame filled Europe, and his evangelical
views, spread by his scholars, prepared the
way for Wycliffe and others who were to come
after him. Light began to dawn with this great
man.

Black Death

In 1348 this fearful pestilence broke out. It was one of the most destructive in history. Appearing first in Asia, it came west, crossing Europe with "terror marching before it, and death following in its rear". On 1st August the plague reached England. "Beginning at Dorchester," says Fox, "every day twenty, some days forty, some fifty, and more, dead corpses were brought and laid together in one deep pit." On 1st November it reached London, "where the vehement rage thereof was so hot, and did increase so much, that from the first day of February till about the beginning of May, in a church-yard then newly made by Smithfield (Charterhouse), about two hundred dead corpses every day were buried, besides those which in other church-yards of the city were laid also". "In those days," says another, "scarcely were there left living folk for to bury honestly them that were dead." 100,000 died in London and half of the entire nation was struck down – nowhere escaped. Animals were also affected and putrid carcases covered the fields. Farm labourers stopped work; the law courts were closed, and Parliament too. Terror, mourning and death reigned.

Wycliffe's Conversion

He had seen the terrible result of the destroyer and was deeply affected. Two-thirds of his native county, the West Riding of Yorkshire, perished. It appeared that the end of the world was at hand. "This visitation of the Almighty," says d'Aubigne, "sounded like the trumpet of the judgement-day in the heart of Wycliffe." He had been brought to the Bible by Bradwardine, and the plague brought him to it again, but with a terrible sense of need. Now he studied it more earnestly than ever, not as the theologian, but as a seeking soul. The Black Death made him seek a refuge from judgement to come: the Word of God pointed to Christ.

His Parents

It appears from Wycliffe's own writings that he could well have been rejected by his parents after his conversion, when he began to attack the abuses of the Church, and then the Church itself. In his own words he says, "If a child yield himself to meekness and poverty and flee covetousness and pride from a dread of sin and to please God... they [his parents] curse him because he liveth well and will teach other men the will of God to save their souls. For by so doing the child getteth many enemies among his elders, and they say that he slandereth all their noble kindred who were held true men and worshipful [honourable]." He was obviously describing his own bitter experience. He learned from an early age to stand alone! Other sources confirm the hostility of his family to his doctrine.

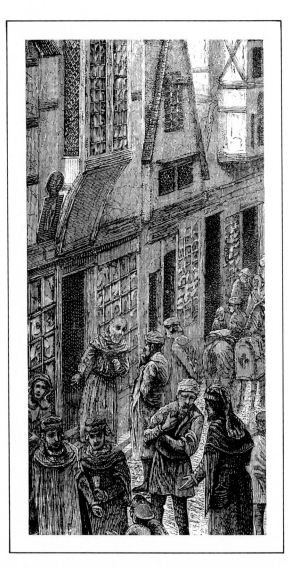

Oxford street scene

Academic Life

He had gone to Oxford when he was 16, first to Queen's then to Merton. Merton is the oldest college in Oxford, dating from 1264. In 1356, while he was still at this college (before he became Master of Balliol), he is thought by some to have written a famous treatise entitled 'The Last Age of the Church'. In it the writer considered the plague to have been a righteous scourge for the prevailing vices of the age.

Between the years 1356 and 1360 he was elected the third Master of Balliol, and soon after given the comfortable living of Fillingham in Lincolnshire. This meant he had to resign his Mastership, but did not leave the University. He hired lodgings in Queen's College and, later, briefly he became Warden of Canterbury Hall. It is evident that he loved Oxford because in one of his rare personal reminiscences, writing in a letter composed while at Lutterworth, he burst into a rhapsody on the town of Oxford, the beauty of its site and its wooded, watery setting. However, his enormous industry could have left him little time for anything else but study. He never held an important office in the University itself, but enjoyed enormous prestige and, according to MacFarlane, deserved it. Even his enemies agreed that he was "the flower of

Oxford; in philosophy second to none, without a rival in the discipline of the schools".

Archbishop Arundel, the enemy of the Lollards (Wycliffe's followers), said of him, "Wycliffe was a great clerk, and many held him a perfect liver." No one of his many detractors ever accused him of incontinence or self-indulgence. Pride and disappointed ambition are the charges made. He was a disciple of Roger Bacon, 'Dr. Mirabilis', who had lived at Oxford until 1292, and had grasped and exemplified the experimental method of science. Wycliffe's sermons reveal how broad his studies must have been. They include references to the law of optics, chemical analysis, physiological genesis of sleep, geometrical and arithmetical rules, and national economics. It appears from the success with which he was able to gather round him a group of able young scholars that he had a gift for inspiring academic discipleship. Although, like Calvin, he had a meagre physique, his earnestness, undeniable learning, single-mindedness and personal simplicity made him a dominant figure in the University.

Learning from Others

While at Oxford he was greatly impressed with the writings of Robert Grosetete, Bishop of Lincoln, who had had a great influence on the University, and was deeply concerned about the moral condition of the country and the Church. However, he advanced on Grosetete by attacking not only the *life* but the *doctrine* of the church. William Occam had light with regard to the authority of Scripture, but again, Wycliffe took his doctrine further. Thomas Bradwardine, Archbishop of Canterbury, 'Dr. Profundis', delivered lectures at Oxford which influenced him. Here again Wycliffe was prepared to disagree where he felt this was necessary. He was helped by Augustine and rejected Pelagius' system of theology, but did not follow Augustine altogether, believing that original sin is not transmitted physically, but through the mind. What Wycliffe read had to go through the fine sieve of his critical mind.

Wycliffe grew up to maturity surrounded by bad examples and gross spiritual darkness. There were, however, a few to guide him; above all, he had the Word of God, albeit in Latin. It set him free, and became his guiding light. He was not to hide it under a bushel. For Wycliffe, the Word of God had to be proclaimed and applied. When once he saw a truth it had to be declared and acted upon. This led him inevitably into conflict, and the rest of his life was one of struggle and labour, but of great usefulness extending far beyond Oxford. The enormous effect of his industry and faith is hard to measure, but some outstanding tributes have been paid to him through the ages.

His Influence on England Greater than Luther

Wycliffe did more than any other man to change the course of English history. His influence upon the English Reformation has been greatly underestimated. We are accustomed to assuming that Luther did more for England than Wycliffe but the opposite is the case. The testimony of John Fox in his

John Fox

'Book of Martyrs' may come as a surprise to us. He describes the condition of this land . . .

before the name of Luther was heard of among the people in these countries.

Wherefore, they are much misinformed which condemn this kind of doctrine, now received, as being new, asking, Where was this church and religion before Luther's time? To whom it may be answered, that this religion and form of doctrine, first planted by the apostles, afterwards decayed, and now reformed again, although it was not received or admitted by the Pope's clergy before Luther's time, neither yet is received, was received by others, in whose hearts it pleased the Lord secretly to work, and that of a great number who both professed and suffered for the same.

We then have, from the same reliable source, a most remarkable testimony of the strength of Wycliffe's followers on the eve of the Reformation.

The church in England hath not lacked great multitudes, which tasted and followed the sweetness of God's holy word, almost in as ample manner, as now. Although public authority to maintain the open preaching of the gospel then was wanting, yet the secret multitude of true professors was not much unequal. Certainly, the fervent zeal of those christian days seemed much superior to these our days and times, as manifestly may appear by their sitting up all night in reading and hearing. Also by their expenses and charges in buying books in English; some gave a load of hay for a few chapters of St James or of St Paul in English.

I greatly marvel and muse to consider how the word of truth did multiply so exceedingly among them. Wherein is to be seen, no doubt, the marvellous working of God's mighty power. For so I find and observe in considering the registers, how one neighbour resorting and conferring with another, soon did win and persuade their minds to that wherein they desired to persuade them, touching the truth of God's word and his sacraments. To see their travails, their earnest seeking, their burning zeal, their readings, their watchings, their sweet assemblies, their love and concord, their godly living, their marrying with the faithful, *may make us now in these our days of free profession to blush for shame*. [Italics mine]

Father of the English Reformation

This quotation is of the utmost importance. It is crucial to our estimate of the value of Wycliffe's work and should greatly increase our interest in this man. John Wycliffe is known as the Morning Star of the Reformation but has been described by Dr. Robert Vaughan as "the *father* of the English Reformation". He has also been described by Professor McFarlane as the one to whom "English Non-conformity *owes its origins*." The Lollards, Wycliffe's followers, were the forerunners of the Baptists and Independents. Wycliffe not only laid the foundation of the Reformation in this country, but that of Puritanism and Non-conformity. This will become clear through the pages of this book, from his own writings and from the historic evidence of recent research. His great success is to be measured not by the reforms he achieved in the political and ecclesiastical scene, but by the effect of his evangelistic labours, which bore fruit in "due season".

A Personal Tribute

Professor Burrows, who delivered lectures before the University of Oxford just prior to the 500th anniversary of Wycliffe's death, tells us, in common with most of his biographers, that Wycliffe's place in history has been greatly underestimated. This has arisen partly because his own works were written before the advent of printing and few copies survived the flames in England. Of those that had been preserved on the Continent, few were made available to the general public until the nineteenth century. The publication of his works then had a considerable effect upon the estimate made of his worth. "The country for which he lived and died is only beginning to wake up to the sense of that debt it owes his memory. And yet so vast is that debt, so overpowering the claim, that it might be thought no very extravagant recognition if every town in England had a monument to his memory, and every university a college named in his honour."

Burrows goes on, in the usual style of Wycliffe's biographers, to describe the part he played in the English Reformation, a part that has been greatly undervalued. He acknowledges the importance of the Renaissance, the struggle in Germany and of Henry VIII in bringing about the great event in England: but he calls upon us to give full weight to the work that had been going on **beneath the surface** since Wycliffe's time through his works, and asserts that without a knowledge of this fact we could not understand the English Reformation.

Since such tributes were paid in the last century only occasional interest has been shown in Wycliffe. In the last fifty years Wycliffe has almost been forgotten, at a time when he most needs to be remembered. The cover of this book is a copy of the painting, 'Dawn of the Reformation'. This illustrates the point we are making. He was more than a 'Morning Star', and it was his preachers that were especially used. Wycliffe's great strength was his attachment to the Scriptures. It was this sword, that he and his preachers

wielded so well, that accomplished so much.

The 'Evangelical Doctor'

What was characteristic of the man, more than anything else, was his submission to the Bible as the Word of God. He would be called a Fundamentalist today in his attitude to the literal text of Scripture. Intellectually he was second to none, but had a child-like faith. The title given to him, the 'Evangelical Doctor' (Doctor of the Gospel), is the highest tribute we can pay to him. All his usefulness derived from his respect for the Word of God. To him the Word of God was the voice of God and the power of God. It transformed him, and through him transformed others. They adopted his view of the Scriptures and carried it right through to the Reformation itself.

Though he was an academic, he was not a mere intellectual. His deep experience of the power of God comes through in his writings. He could not have withstood the tremendous opposition he faced without a deep experience of the grace of God. His frequent reference to the "bliss of heaven" tells us that he must have known Divine support when he stood increasingly alone. There were many lesser men who supported him, but none other could do the work he did in his conflict with the powers of darkness – and things were indeed dark in his day.

2.

The Struggle Begins.

As Wycliffe grew spiritually, so he grew in his awareness of the moral corruption and spiritual confusion that was about him. He never hesitated throughout his life to expose and denounce that which dishonoured God. But he was not alone. Things were so bad that it was common for the Church and its institutions, and clerics in general, to be criticised. We referred to Chaucer's 'Canterbury Tales', in which Chaucer lays bare the rottenness of the Church's agents. The famous 'Vision of Piers Ploughman' forcefully unmasked the sins of the clergy, but the poem itself assumed that the body of Church doctrine was basically sound. Those who went before Wycliffe certainly prepared the way, but they did not go nearly far enough. They all attacked the life of the Church, but not its doctrine and institutions as a whole. Furthermore, there were excellent men like Fitzralph, Archbishop of Armargh, Grosetete and Bradwardine, who were spiritually enlightened on vital issues, but none of them attacked the Church as an institution.

Fundamental Reforms Necessary

Wycliffe's mind developed. He compared everything he saw about him with the Scriptures and gradually realized that the whole system of Rome was at variance with the Word of God. He came to this point, according to Fox, not without tears and groans.

After he had a long time professed divinity in Oxford, and perceiving the true doctrine of Christ's Gospel to be adulterate, and defiled with so many filthy inventions of bishops, sects of monks, and dark errors, and after long debating and deliberating with himself (with many secret sighs and bewailings in his mind the general ignorance of the whole world), he could no longer suffer or abide the same, he at the last determined with himself to help and to remedy such things as he saw to be wide and out of the way. But forasmuch as he saw that this dangerous meddling could not be attempted without great troubles, neither that these things, which had been so long time with use and custom rooted and grafted in men's minds, could be suddenly plucked up or taken away, he thought with himself that this matter should be done by little and little. Wherefore he, starting with small things thereby opened himself a way or means to greater matters. First he assailed his adversaries in logical and metaphysical questions . . . by these originals the way was made unto greater points, so that at length he came to touch the matters of the Sacraments, and other abuses of the Church.

No 'Heresy'

Prior to Wycliffe there is no trace of any native 'heresy', ('heresy' as far as the Catholic Church was concerned), neither is there any evidence that the foreign sects found a footing in England, however much they spread on the Continent in the twelfth and thirteenth centuries. Lechler (one of Wycliffe's biographers) pursued this point very carefully and maintained that in all Wycliffe's writings, which he had searched through in manuscript, he never came across a single trace of the appearance of 'heretics' in England. Wycliffe does not so much as refer to the Waldensians of Italy or Albigensians of France. Lechler maintains that there is no support for believing that there were secret disciples of Waldensian doctrine in England in Wycliffe's day. He adds that if there were any foundation for this conjecture, Wycliffe's enemies would most certainly have used it to their own advantage.

This point is of supreme importance because it shows what a great thing it was for Wycliffe to do what no Englishman had ever done before, that is to attack the Church itself. We need to remember that there was no alternative to the Church of Rome: it was *the* Church. Englishmen knew of nothing else and the Church permeated the whole of society. Wycliffe was given incredible boldness, therefore, to call in question the very foundations of this institution that held every Englishman in its grasp. Previous to Wycliffe it was quite compatible to criticise the Church and yet to be devoted to its cause and be in submission to the Pope, as we mentioned earlier in the chapter.

Not Political

There was another way in which he differed from those who went before him. Politicians levelled much criticism at the Church and, as

Begging Friar

we shall see, they were very willing to use Wycliffe when it suited them. But Wycliffe would not act as a political leader – trying to get what political reforms he could. He was concerned simply to spread the truth of God, and looked to God to honour his Word.

The Friars Attacked

Wycliffe began his attack on the medieval Church by exposing the errors and vices of the begging friars. He had begun by showing respect for them because of their beginnings and the life of St Francis. They professed to depend on the gifts of others, but their corruptions had become notorious. In 1360 he published his 'Objections to the Friars'. They had never been so forcibly assaulted before. The vigour of his mind and the conviction of his soul began to be displayed to these enemies of the Gospel and to the common people. The friars realised that they faced a foe who would not relent. It was his pastoral concern for the people that moved him. The friars not only failed to do any good; they did great harm.

His complaint against the friar was that "he **stuffs the people only too effectually with garbage"**. They were expert communicators. They knew how to make a long discourse on the seven deadly sins attractive by telling a long story of a miser carried off by the devil, or a murderer detected in the act. The arts of sensationalism were their stock-in-trade, but what proved their main attraction was the cheap price at which they granted absolution to the people. Wycliffe's contest with the begging friars continued through his life. They were a great nuisance at Oxford where they were in force. They had attacked the laws and privileges of Oxford and claimed independence of the jurisdiction of the University. This brought them into collision with the college authorities, and Fitzralph (who was Chancellor in 1333), described them as "this pestiferous cancer", and appealed to Avignon where the Pope then lived (having moved from Rome), hoping to reform this evil. Fitzralph complained of their doctrine and manner of life, and the general effect on the University: the students could not even find books to carry on their studies; the friars were proselytising from among their ranks and parents of scholars were horrified.

The Contest Between England and the Papacy

England had long been struggling to gain its freedom from Rome ever since the days of King John. This continuing struggle gave Wycliffe a great opportunity to make his views of the Papacy well known so as to undermine its influence. In 1365 Pope Urban V attempted to re-assert the supremacy over England and Parliament which had been achieved in 1213.

We need to go back about 150 years to

King John humbling himself before the Papal Legate

understand the relationship that existed between the English Crown and the Papacy. Early in the thirteenth century, a dispute arose between King John and some of the monks concerning the appointment of the Archbishop of Canterbury. Both sides appealed to Rome, but the Pope took the opportunity to appoint the Archbishop himself, and claimed this right for all time. John was angered because he saw that the Pope might next want the power of appointing to the throne itself.

He defied Rome and ordered the bishops and abbots to leave the kingdom. The Pope struck back by prohibiting all services in church and, after two years, excommunicated him. He also encouraged the French to invade England. John was on bad terms with the barons, and could not count on their support, and so surrendered unconditionally to the Pope, resigning the kingdom to Pope Innocent and his successors, agreeing that his dominions should be held in feud, (i.e. on condition of homage and service to a superior lord).

He agreed to pay annually 1,000 marks, (one mark equalled two thirds of one pound sterling) and that if he or his successors ever broke the agreement they should lose all right to the realm. He actually took off his crown and offered it to the papal legate, putting England into the Pope's hands. This happened on 15th May, 1213. England was never more humiliated. The barons were stung into action: they would never be slaves to the Pope! This was one of the reasons why they forced John to sign the Magna Carta on 15th June, 1215. The Pope denounced the barons, declared the charter null and void and suspended the Archbishop of Canterbury, whom he had appointed himself, for his part in the proceedings.

The Pope Demands Payment

The annual 'rental', which was paid to the Pope for the right to rule England had lapsed, but in 1365 it was demanded. The Pope couldn't have chosen a worse time to demand submission to the 'Holy See'. England was becoming more self-conscious of its achievements and its independence from Europe. The crushing victory over the French at Crecy was fresh in the minds of men, and the King was in no mood to give a thousand marks to the Pope for permission to wear a crown he could defend so well with his sword. He was particularly angered as there were good grounds for believing that this money would find its way from Avignon into the pockets of those who were fighting against our soldiers in France. Edward assembled his parliament in 1366, presented them with the Pope's letter, and asked them to consider the matter. Their response could hardly be in doubt. Had the nation not advanced since the days of John? Could it not go higher under Edward? Wycliffe has preserved for us a

Magna Carta Monument, Runnymede

summary of the speeches, being present on that occasion.

A military baron spoke first. "The kingdom of England was won by the sword, and by that sword has been defended. Let the Pope then gird on his sword, and come and try to exact this tribute by force, and I for one am ready to resist him." A second baron rose to his feet. "He only," said he, "is entitled to secular tribute who legitimately exercises secular rule, and is able to give secular protection. The Pope cannot legitimately do either; he is a minister of the Gospel, not a temporal ruler. His duty is to give spiritual counsel, not corporal protection. Let us see that he abide within the limits of his spiritual office, where we shall obey him; but if he shall choose to transgress these limits, he must take the consequences." "The Pope," said a third, "calls himself the servant of the servants of God. Very well: he can claim recompense only for service done. But where are the services which he renders to this land? Does he minister to us in spirituals? Does he help us in temporals? Does he not rather greedily drain our treasures, and often for the benefit of our enemies? I give my voice against this tribute."

"On what grounds was this tribute originally demanded?" asked another. "Was it not for absolving King John, and relieving the kingdom from interdict? [prohibition of services]. But to bestow spiritual benefits for money is sheer simony; it is a piece of ecclesiastical swindling. Let the lords spiritual and temporal wash their hands of a transaction so disgraceful. But if it is as feudal superior of the kingdom that the Pope demands this tribute, why ask a thousand marks? Why not ask the throne, the soil, the people of England? If his title be good for these thousand marks, it is good for a great deal more. The Pope, on the same principle, may declare the throne vacant, and fill it with whomsoever he pleases." "Pope Urban tells us," – so spoke another – "that all kingdoms are Christ's, and that he as his vicar holds England for Christ; but as the Pope is peccable [capable of sin], and may abuse his trust, it appears to me that it were better that we should hold our land directly and alone of Christ." "Let us," said the last speaker, "go at once to the root of this matter. King John had no right to give away the kingdom of England without the consent of the nation. That consent was never given. The golden seal of the King, and the seals of the few nobles whom John persuaded or coerced to join him in this transaction, do not constitute the national consent. If John gifted his subjects to Innocent like so many chattels, Innocent may come and take his property if he can. We the people of England had no voice in the matter; we hold the bargain null and void from the beginning."

Parliament was unanimous:

> Forasmuch as neither King John, nor any other king, could bring his realm and kingdom into such thraldom and subjection but by common assent of Parliament, the which was not given, therefore that which he did was against his oath at his coronation, besides many other causes. If, therefore, the Pope should attempt anything against the King, the King, with all his subjects, should, with all their force and power, resist the same.

Wycliffe's Influence

Wycliffe had largely brought about this state of feeling in England, and he had taught the barons and Commons. He gave resolution to those only too willing to use his arguments. It is clear that Wycliffe was already having a great influence, not only because the politicians were using his arguments, but because a monk defended the Pope's actions and called upon Wycliffe to disprove his propositions. We do not know who he was, but he argued in favour of the Pope's claim. He asserted that,

'as vicar of Christ, the Pope is the feudal superior of monarchs, and the lord paramount of their kingdoms.' Thence he deduced the following conclusions:- 'that all sovereigns owe him obedience and tribute; that vassalage was specially due from the English monarch in consequence of the surrender of the kingdom to the Pope by John; that Edward had clearly forfeited his throne by the non-payment of the annual tribute; and, in fine, that all ecclesiastics, regulars and seculars, were exempt from the civil jurisdiction, and under no obligation to obey the citation or answer before the tribunal of the magistrate.' (Wylie).

Wycliffe responded. It was not hard to answer the arguments, but he was attacking the greatest power on earth. The battle had begun. He started his assault on the Pope on behalf of England. England was prepared for this; but he would carry the battle further than the politicians desired or expected – even when they deserted him. He began by styling himself 'the King's peculiar clerk', from which we gather that the King had taken notice of him and made him a chaplain. **"Already,"** he said, **"a third and more of England is in the hands of the Pope. There cannot be two temporal sovereigns in one country; either Edward is king or Urban is king. We make our choice. We accept Edward of England and refuse Urban of Rome."** It was a masterstroke to demonstrate that the quarrel was not between an unknown monk and an Oxford doctor, but between the King of England and the Pontiff of Rome. It was a crucial moment. Would the victor of the battle of Crecy do homage to Urban for his crown? If England bowed before Rome, what monarch could hope to stand erect? What country could free itself from the bondage of Rome?

At about this time, Wycliffe had appealed to Rome because his wardenship of Canterbury Hall, to which he was appointed, had been taken from him by Archbishop Langham. It is not surprising that his appeal failed. He lost his wardenship, but helped to save the independency of his country. Soon after this he took his degree of Doctor of Divinity – a rare distinction in his day.

Bruges

The Battle Continues

The contest between England and Rome was to continue. The battle was far from over. It was just beginning. Two famous statutes, of 'Provisors and Praemunire', had been passed. These were intended to stop the Pope taking possession of wealthy, lucrative benefices (i.e. well paid positions in the church) in England, and to shut the door against tithes, revenues and other sources of money that flowed from England to the Vatican. The very best of English benefices and dignities were occupied by Italians, Frenchmen and other foreigners. Some of them were, "mere boys and not only ignorant of the English language but even of Latin, and who never so much as saw their churches but committed care of them to those they could get to serve them the cheapest, and had the revenues of them sent to them at Rome or elsewhere".

The two laws were ineffective, and Parliament urged the King to do something about it. Accordingly, in 1373, the King sent commissioners to Avignon to Pope Gregory XI, but the ambassadors got nowhere. Parliament complained again, and urged that "remedy be provided against the provisions of the Pope whereby he reaps the firstfruits of ecclesiastical dignities, the treasure of the realm being thereby conveyed away, which they cannot bear". When a Royal Commission enquired into the number of benefices and dignities held by foreigners they discovered that the clergy of England was rapidly becoming alien and nominal, and the sums drained away from the realm were enormous.

Wycliffe has a Glimpse of Rome

The King tried again. This time he sent four commissioners, one of whom was John Wycliffe. The fact that his name appears second on the list of delegates indicates his growing influence. This time the Pope sent his nuncios to receive the delegates at Bruges in the Netherlands. The negotiations got bogged down for two years, and then the result was a compromise. It left the Pope with equal power over the benefices of England to that of the sovereign. The Pope did not renounce his right but simply gave assurance that he would not exercise it. This was most unsatisfactory because no sooner had the commissioners returned home than the Pope carried on as before. There was a suspicion of betrayal because the Bishop of Bangor, who took a leading part in the negotiations, immediately became Bishop of Hereford. His promotion was the result of the use of papal power.

Wycliffe came home feeling that he had wasted two years, but he had learned a great deal. His contact with the confidants of the Pope had a similar effect on him to Luther's famous visit to Rome. He had met those who were in the closest contact with the Pope and the cardinals, and the lessons were not lost on him. He could see through them what principles reigned in the papal court, and what motives guided its policy. He did not meet the Pope himself, but he could read him in his servants. This is evident because in his public lectures he now spoke of the Pope as **"Anti-Christ, the proud, worldly priest of Rome and the most cursed of clippers and purse-kervers".** In one of his tracts he adds, **"They [the Pope and his collectors] draw out of our land poor men's livelihoods and many thousand marks by the year of the King's money for sacraments and spiritual things that is cursed heresy and simony, and maketh all Christendom assent and maintain his heresy."**

It would appear that he himself was rewarded for his conduct at Bruges because he was soon appointed Rector of Lutterworth, which appointment did not come from the Pope, but the King.

Firmer Action

Parliament decided that they must do something more definite because the Pope received five times more than the King in revenue. They drew up a Bill of Indictment against the Pope: "God hath given his sheep to the Pope to be pastored and not shorn and shaven . . . therefore it would be good to renew all the statutes against provisions from Rome . . . No papal collector should remain in England upon pain of life and limb, and no Englishman, on the like pain, should become such collector or remain at the court of Rome."

It would appear that Wycliffe was behind this bold move. He was intensely patriotic and his convictions at this point were in line with those of Parliament. His style is recognisable in the document of Parliament. The Pope was furious and, in defiance, appointed an Italian to an English benefice - but Parliament stood firm: "We will support the crown against the tiara." The lords likewise affirmed the royal prerogative against papal power. The nation supported the Estates of the Realm and called this parliament 'The Good Parliament'. This was, indeed, a great victory. In an age that Crecy and Poitiers made so famous, this victory was even greater and more long-lasting. Wycliffe became a national champion but he was soon to pay the price.

3.

In the Arena.

Wycliffe Attacked Personally

Wycliffe's influence was growing. He could see more clearly the Papacy for what it was. He used his position at Oxford, and at Lutterworth, and his influence with those in Parliament with whom he had close contact, but opposition was bound to come. The friars were already furious with him, but now the Church hierarchy were angry, too. He had defended England against Rome, but had stirred up a hornet's nest. The Church was not used to this treatment but knew what to do. Fox sums up what happened: "The whole glut of monks and begging friars were set in rage or madness which did assail this good man on every side, fighting for their altars, paunches and bellies. After them the priests, and then after them the Archbishop took the matter in hand."

Wycliffe must be struck down. His writings were examined and there was plenty that they could seize upon with which to condemn him. He had taught that the Pope has no more power than ordinary priests to excommunicate or absolve men; that princes cannot give endowments forever to the Church; that when their gifts are abused they can recall them; and that Christ gave no temporal lordship to the popes or supremacies over kings.

On May 22nd, 1377, three papal 'bulls' (decrees) were sent to England. The English clergy were chastised for allowing this "dangerous heresy" to spring up on their soil, and were urged to take immediate steps to silence Wycliffe. The first bull was sent to Sudbury, the Archbishop, and William Courtenay, Bishop of London, and the second to the King, and the third to Oxford.

The Pope condemned Wycliffe as "a master of errors" who "had run into a kind of detestable wickedness, not only openly publishing but also vomiting out of the filthy dungeon of his breast false and erroneous conclusions and most wicked and damnable heresies whereby he might defile the faithful and bring them headlong into perdition". On the Pope's authority, Wycliffe was to be shut up in prison and proofs of his heresy made secure until further instructions were given.

Uproar in St. Paul's

The English bishops didn't wait for the bulls to arrive. Courtenay acted quickly and called Wycliffe to appear before him in St. Paul's on 19th February, 1377. News travelled and a great crowd gathered at the door. Wycliffe had at his side two powerful friends, John of Gaunt (Duke of Lancaster), and Lord Percy (Earl Marshal of England). John of Gaunt had probably met Wycliffe at Bruges where they were on different missions at the same time. He held the Reformer in high esteem on political grounds. His opinions coincided with Wycliffe's on national issues and he was anxious to use him in his quarrel against the Church. Wycliffe appeared in the presence of his judges, "a meagre form, dressed in a long, light mantle of black cloth similar to those worn by doctors, ministers and students in Cambridge and Oxford, with a girdle round his waist. His face showed

John of Gaunt

sharp, bold features, a clear, piercing eye, firmly closed lips; his whole appearance full of great earnestness of character."

The three friends found it difficult to find their way through the crowd. A disturbance took place in the process. Percy was the first to get into the Lady Chapel, and Courtenay was angry, most likely at seeing Wycliffe so powerfully befriended. He addressed Percy: "If I had known what masteries you would have kept in the church I would have stopped you from coming in hither." John of Gaunt interrupted, having arrived himself: "He shall keep such masteries, though you say nay." Percy then told Wycliffe to sit down – "Sit down, Wycliffe. You have many things to answer to and have need to repose yourself on a soft seat." "He must and shall stand." said Courtenay, still more heated. "It is unreasonable that one on his trial should sit." "Lord Percy's proposal is but reasonable," interrupted Gaunt, "and as for you," he added, addressing Courtenay, "who are grown so arrogant and proud, I will bring down the pride not of you alone but of all the prelacy in England." The bishop calmly replied that his trust was not in any friend on earth but in God. John of Gaunt got more angry and the exchanges hotter, till Gaunt was heard to say "rather than take such words from the bishop he would drag him out of the court by the hair of his head". This heated debate was of great interest to the crowd who burst, en masse, into the chapel. It all became an uproar. The trial was abandoned, the bishops had to retreat and Wycliffe returned home. "And so," says a witness, "their council being broken up with scolding and brawling was dissolved before 9 o'clock."

Parliament Consults Wycliffe

In the providence of God, Wycliffe continued to be protected. Edward III died on 1st June the same year. His renowned son, the Black Prince, had preceded him to the grave, leaving as heir his eleven-year-old son, who became Richard II. The Black Prince's widow was friendly to Wycliffe and unafraid to make her position known. The new parliament was not much different in its composition from the 'Good Parliament', and sought Wycliffe's help. His influence was growing still further. While the papal bulls were still on their way, Parliament showed its confidence in Wycliffe by asking him the following question: "Whether the Kingdom of England might not lawfully in case of necessity detain and keep back the treasure of the kingdom for its defence, that it be not carried away to foreign and strange nations, the Pope himself demanding and requiring the same under pain of censure?" They needed the assurance of Wycliffe, the man of God, that they could stand up to the Pope without incurring sin by disobedience. Parliament had been particularly angered by the way in which money that was needed to carry on wars against the French was going to a Pope who was living in France, and who would support their enemies.

Wycliffe's reply was brief and plain. He based it on the Scriptures. The gold was unquestionably England's, to be retained for its use and defence. If it was objected that the Pope was God's vice-regent, supreme proprietor of all temporalities in Christendom, the question should be asked, "Who gave him this power?" Wycliffe did not find it in the Bible and Peter himself possessed no temporal lordship. The Pope should choose between apostleship and kingship. If he preferred to be a king, let him claim nothing of us in the character of an apostle; or if he was an apostle, he could not claim money. What England gave to the Papacy should not be given as tribute but as alms, and alms could not be demanded unless there was need. Was the Papacy poor? Let charity begin at home. Thus the Reformer led his countrymen, step by step, in their conflict with Rome.

Confidence in God

God, in his sovereignty, allowed Wycliffe to become a national hero. Trevelyan marks off 1378 as the high point of his influence. From then onwards he was to lose popularity.

His influence upon the nation in the political realm diminished – unregenerate men could only be led so far. But his spiritual influence grew. At the peak of his power he was still trusting in the Sovereign God, and well knew that the fickle multitude could easily change its attitude. When, at a later date, he attacked transubstantiation and John of Gaunt rushed to Oxford to tell him to keep quiet, Wycliffe had no difficulty whatever in pursuing his course. Though he had been supported by the most powerful forces in the country, he had not *depended* upon them but on the One who has all authority in heaven and on earth. As his political friends deserted him and as, eventually, he stood alone, he found strength to do this. Indeed, his courage and boldness increased, his faith shone more brightly, and more and more spiritual light illumined his soul. Other Reformers have hesitated, equivocated, and even declined, when political support wavered. This marks Wycliffe out, and gives us reason to see why he accomplished so much in the remaining six years of his life.

4.

He loses favour with Men.

Wycliffe's enemies would not easily give up the fight. Though frustrated, they were all the more determined to deal with the man who was undermining their position. His influence on Parliament was growing, and he had become a national hero. His intellectual brilliance, integrity and fearlessness made him a formidable foe. He understood the papal system, and was leading Parliament and the nation in directions they were not fully aware of. They increasingly denied the political claims of Rome, unaware of the fact that at the same time they were undermining its spiritual authority.

Tried at Lambeth Palace

The arrival of the papal bulls in England gave the ecclesiastical hierarchy the opportunity they wanted; but a shield still protected Wycliffe. To the very end he was given the strength and opportunity to fulfill the work he was called to do. The bull addressed to the King, found Edward in the grave. The one sent to Oxford was treated with disdain – they were unlikely to put out the light of their greatest scholar! The bishops, however, acted without delay.

Wycliffe was called to appear before the Primate in April, 1378. The court sat at Lambeth. Wycliffe was accused not only of reviving errors, but adding new ones of his own and was to be dealt with as though he were "a common thief". The bishops approached the matter with caution – Wycliffe had too many friends. This was evident when he arrived, because a crowd, quite as large and more friendly than the one which besieged St Paul's, surrounded the Palace of Lambeth. He was still a national

Wycliffe entering Lambeth Palace supported by a large crowd of people who followed him inside

hero, though few understood how far-reaching his plans for reform were. No sooner had he entered the chapel than the crowd came in after him, filling the space and making their sympathies evident to the bishops.

While the bishops were considering the best way to deal with these unwelcome spectators, Sir Richard Clifford entered with a message from the Queen Mother, the widow of the Black Prince, forbidding them to pass sentence upon Wycliffe. The effect was dramatic! "At the wind of a reed shaken," says Walsingham, "their speech became soft as oil to the public loss of their own dignity and the damage of the whole Church. They were struck with such a dread that you would think them to be as a man that heareth not and in whose mouth are no reproofs." Wycliffe remained calm. Again he escaped unhurt from the hands of his enemies. He took the opportunity, however, to make his position known. The forthrightness of the man is astonishing, bearing in mind the hostility of his judges.

Wycliffe's Boldness

In the lengthy written defence, which he handed to his judges, he declared that the popes have no political authority but only spiritual, and their spiritual authority is not absolute. They may fall into sin like others, and ought to be reproved. The Pope has no supremacy over temporal possessions and priests have no power to absolve men unless it is accompanied by the pardon of God. Excommunication hurts no one unless they have provoked God's anger. In his denial of the Pope's power to excommunicate, and the priests' power to absolve from sin, he challenged the fundamental power of the Church. He was comprehensive in his attack. He asserted that the Church did not have any property in a strict or legal sense. Her vast acres, that covered half the face of England, were neither purchased nor won by service. She had no right to possess such domains. She was but the administrator of this property. If she mis-used it the nation was bound to withdraw it from her.

Wycliffe even denied that tithes could be claimed. He considered that the Old Testament provision of one tenth for the support of the priests was no longer binding. While he recognised the words of the Apostle, "Let him that is taught in the Word minister to him that teaches in all good things", he denied the right of priests to insist on support if they failed in their office. "Prelates are more bound to preach truly the Gospel than their subjects are to pay tithes. They are more accursed who cease from their preaching than are their subjects who cease to pay tithes even while their prelates do their office well."

Nothing could restrain Wycliffe from declaring broadly, boldly and plainly the reforms that needed to be carried through if the Church was to prosper. There is no trace of hesitation in the clear stand he took, even to the very last moment of his life, but his boldness was strengthening the determination of his enemies to deal with him.

Divine Protection

His enemies were resolved to silence him once and for all, but yet again, they were frustrated; this time by two important events. Gregory XI had returned from Avignon to Rome a little while before, only to die (1378). As a result the commission of delegates which was to try Wycliffe had to be dissolved. Edward III, who was too weak to resist Courtenay, Bishop of London, also died, and John of Gaunt, Wycliffe's friend, became Regent.

The Inquisition

There is a very important point that most historians have missed. It relates to the Inquisition (The 'Holy' Office). It has been pointed out that the Pope, in issuing his bulls against Wycliffe, had a deeper, far more serious matter in mind. It was a deliberate effort to establish in England the Papal Inquisition. The Pope wanted the power to arrest Wycliffe himself and try him at Rome. He failed in this, but his successors continued to press their claim for the next 300 years.

Though 'heresy' was pursued in this country for 200 years it was always through the ecclesiastical courts and the law of the land, never by Papal Inquisition and Papal Warrant. Trevelyan gives Wycliffe the credit for this victory over the Pope. It could have been far worse for English 'heretics'.

The Papal Schism (1378)

A third event, of far-reaching character, diverted the malice of Wycliffe's enemies away from his person. When the cardinals met to elect a successor to Gregory the majority, being Frenchmen, wanted a French pope; but now the Papacy was back in Rome, the Roman people did not want the papal court to return again to Avignon. The populace gathered around the hall and threatened that unless they got a Roman for their pope no cardinal would escape alive! The cardinals complied and elected an Italian pope, but once they had escaped from Rome, met again and chose a Frenchman, declaring that they had previously acted under duress. This was the cause of the famous schism which lasted a full half-century, and scandalised Christendom. These two infallible heads were now fighting each other. Each claimed to be the Vicar of Christ on earth. Pope Urban VI at Rome excommunicated his rival, Clement VII at Avignon, and the Pope at Avignon excommunicated the impostor at Rome. They each cursed one another, and hurled upon

Avignon

their rivals terrible anathemas.

It became obvious to Wycliffe that the whole papal system was Anti-christian. He declared the Pope to be the Man of Sin who "exalteth himself above God", II Thessalonians 2:3,4. The Pope was consistently and always Anti-Christ "forasmuch as through his decrees God's commandments, by his commandments, Christ's commandments, by his decretals Paul's Epistles, by his canon law, the canonical Scriptures were vilified, nullified,

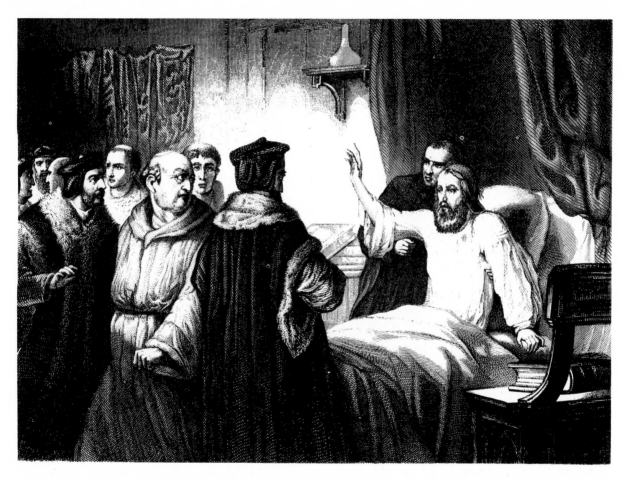

Wycliffe near death

utterly defaced and debased, the Pope is potissimus Antichristis – most especially Anti-Christ". Needless to say, Luther was later grateful for such quotations from Wycliffe's writings.

Near to Death

Wycliffe was now feeling the effects not only of age but of his increasing labours and trials. He fell sick. His enemies, the friars, were overjoyed and hoped he would recant before he died. Delegates from the four Orders hastened to his bedside. "They began fair", wishing him "health and restoration from his distemper", but soon changed their voice. "You have death on your lips." they said. "Be touched by your faults and retract in our presence all that you have said to our injury." Wycliffe was calm, and let them finish all they had to say then, asking his servant to raise him a little on his pillow, though feeble and finding it hard to support himself, he fixed his eyes on them and said with emphasis, **"I shall not die but live and again declare the evil deeds of the friars."** They rushed out of the room in astonishment and confusion. This prophecy was fulfilled: he recovered and devoted the remaining years of his life to his most important work – the propagation of Biblical doctrine; the translation of the Bible; and the sending out of his preachers.

Denial of Transubstantiation

Wycliffe's mind was continually being enlightened by the Scriptures, and in the spring of 1381 he directly assaulted the dogma of transubstantiation. He made twelve propositions public and challenged those who disagreed with him to a debate. In these propositions he declared that: **"The consecrated host which we see on the altar is neither Christ nor any part of him but the efficacious sign of him."** He goes on: **"No pilgrim upon earth is able to see Christ in the consecrated host with the bodily eye, but by faith."** He did not believe that (according to the Doctrine of Transubstantiation) the words of the priest changed the substance of the bread and wine into the actual body and blood of Christ – they are still bread and wine after their consecration. Since Christ called the elements "bread" and "my body", he considered, therefore, that the bread was Christ's body both figuratively and spiritually. He declared plainly that transubstantiation "cannot be shown to have any foundation in the Word of God".

Wycliffe Condemned

The reaction was predictable. No one took up the challenge but all regarded him as an heretic. The Chancellor of the University summoned a council and condemned him, and threatened penalties on any who should teach these things in the University, or listen to such teaching. It met in haste and in secret, and Wycliffe was unaware of what was happening. He did not know of their decision until he was interrupted in a lecture he was giving to his students on the Lord's Supper. A messenger appeared and read out the sentence. He was told to be silent on the subject of transubstantiation and threatened with imprisonment, suspension and excommunication. He was virtually expelled. Wycliffe complained, **"But you ought first to have shown me that I am in error."** The response was simply to repeat the sentence of the court. **"Then,"** said Wycliffe, **"I appeal to the King and to the Parliament."** This was a wise move by Wycliffe. He recognised the importance of maintaining the supremacy of Parliament over ecclesiastical courts.

He Loses Favour With Men

In appealing to Parliament, Wycliffe could not have expected a great deal of support, though he would be certain of more sympathy from that quarter than from the bishops. His support from the secular authorities, however, was diminishing. His patron, John of Gaunt, was alarmed at his views on transubstantiation. Wycliffe was a useful ally in furthering his political ambitions, but would be a liability if he went too far in his attack on the Church. He hurried to Oxford and warned Wycliffe to be silent on the matter, but was told that this was out of the question. John of Gaunt left Oxford baffled. Wycliffe was sacrificing the support from John of Gaunt and Parliament that had been such a help to him, but this cast him entirely on the Lord, and there was no going back. It was the most crucial moment in his life, after his conversion, but he was prepared for it and knew he could not go back on what he had said. His influence with the politicians would diminish but his usefulness in spiritual matters increase greatly. He was as unfettered by human considerations as he had ever been.

Wycliffe's appeal to the King and Parliament gave him time because it was some while before Parliament would meet. He felt, nevertheless, that it would be wise to withdraw to Lutterworth for a time. The University authorities could not follow him to his parish. It was inevitable, however, that the bishops would be after him.

The Peasants Revolt

Later in the same year (1381), the Peasants' Revolt took place. The violence shook the nation. The mob captured the Primate, Sudbury, and beheaded him. Wycliffe was blamed for the revolt, but it is clear that he was not in any way responsible. Certainly, many of the things that he said would lead men to recognise that the long-established institutions could be challenged, and that people should think for themselves, but no one could charge Wycliffe with any implication in the event. Nevertheless, the incident was seized upon in order to blacken his character and to frighten the authorities. It certainly proved a setback as far as Wycliffe was concerned. In particular, it meant that William Courtenay, the Bishop of London, became the Primate. Wycliffe's old enemy now had the power he desired, and was quick to use it.

Blackfriars Synod

Courtenay had to wait until he had authority from Rome before he could act, but did so by calling the Blackfriars' Synod. On 17th May, 1382, the court met in the monastery of Blackfriars. Eight prelates, fourteen doctors, six Bachelors of Divinity, four monks and fifteen friars took their seats. Then the whole building began to rock, and the whole city of London was shaken by a powerful earthquake. Huge stones fell out of castle walls and pinnacles toppled.

Wycliffe called it a judgement of God and afterwards described the gathering as the 'Earthquake Council'. Courtenay on the other hand interpreted it differently.

This earthquake portends the purging of the kingdom from heresies, for as there are shut up in the bowels of the earth many noxious spirits which are expelled in an earthquake, and so the earth is cleansed but not without great violence, so there are many heresies shut up in the hearts of reprobate men, but by the condemnation of them, the kingdom is to be cleansed; but not without irksomeness and great commotion.

The court was persuaded by his words and continued with the trial of Wycliffe. Twenty-six propositions, selected from his writings, were read out. They condemned ten as heretical, and the remainder as erroneous. Their conclusions were published to the bishops, who declared that Wycliffe's doctrines were forbidden in their dioceses. Courtenay was determined to deal with Oxford, which was a source of the 'heresy'. However, there was a new Chancellor, Robert Rigge, who sympathised with the Reformer.

He was obliged therefore, to complain to the young Richard II: "If we permit this heretic to appeal continually to the passions of the people, our destruction is inevitable. We must silence these Lollards." The King gave him authority "to confine to the prisons of the State any who should maintain the condemned propositions". Many of Wycliffe's Oxford friends deserted him rather than expose themselves to danger. He became more and more isolated, but did not shrink from his task. He had supporters in high places, but few who would openly take his side.

Appeal to Parliament

The following year, on 19th November, he had his opportunity to appeal to Parliament. He called for sweeping changes. He insisted that those in monastic Orders should be released from unnatural and immoral vows which had made them the scandal of the Church. "Since Jesus Christ shed his blood to free his church, I demand its freedom. I demand that everyone may leave these gloomy walls within which a tyrannical law prevails, and embrace a simple and peaceful life under the vault of heaven."

His second point dealt with the possessions of the Church. Wycliffe believed that the main reason why the Church was so corrupt was because of its great wealth. He called for the State to take possession of the property of the Church that was really under the jurisdiction of the King.

His third point had to do with tithes and offerings. They should only be given according to the needs of the recipients that they might discharge their duties. If priests were found to be unworthy they should not receive support.

I demand that the poor inhabitants of our towns and villages be not constrained to furnish a worldly priest, often a vicious man and a heretic, with the means of satisfying his ostentation, his gluttony and his licentiousness, by buying a showy horse, costly saddles, bridles with dangling bells, rich garments and soft furs, while they see the wives and children of their neighbours dying with hunger.

(Well might Chaucer have remembered these words when giving us, not long after, his pen picture of the clerical pilgrims!)

His fourth point dealt with transubstantiation, which he believed was particularly dangerous. He considered that the doctrine of the 'real presence' being understood in a physical sense was satanic in its origin. He pictures Satan as reasoning thus:

Should I once so far beguile the faithful of the Church, by the aid of Anti-Christ my vice-regent, as to persuade them to deny that this Sacrament is bread, but merely looks like it, there will be nothing then which I will not bring them to receive, since there can be nothing more opposite to the Scriptures, or the common discernment. Let the life of a prelate be then what it may, let him be guilty of luxury, simony or murder, the people may be led to believe that he is really no such man — nay, they may then be persuaded to admit that the Pope is infallible, at least with respect to matters of Christian faith: and that,

Wycliffe tried at Oxford

inasmuch as he is known by the name Most Holy Father, he is of course free from sin.

(It was not until 500 years later that the Pope was declared infallible.)

Wycliffe was anxious for men to use their minds while studying the Scriptures. If the Church could impose on men this monstrous belief, there was no limit to what they could persuade men to believe. This assault by Wycliffe on the doctrine and practices of the Church was astounding. His friends had left him, one after the other, and now, surely, he must yield. But the boldness was given him by the One who stood by him when others deserted. To the consternation of his adversaries, the Commons and Parliament repealed the royal edict and Wycliffe thus won his cause.

Trial Before the Convocation at Oxford

Courtenay now had to turn to Convocation: he could be confident of the support of the 'Parliament of the Church'. He gathered six bishops, many Doctors of Divinity and a host of the lower clergy. The meeting took place at Oxford. This was the place where Wycliffe had shone most brightly. He was the jewel of the University that was foremost in Western Europe, yet his judges were anxious to put an end to him once and for all.

They fastened particularly on the matter of transubstantiation. Did he affirm or deny this cardinal doctrine of the Church? It was out of character for Wycliffe to yield or modify his opinions, which had been shown him plainly from the Scriptures, and his response reflected this. His reply was scholarly and detailed, but did not budge for one moment from his clearly-held views – that there was no fleshly presence of Christ in the sacrament, nor any other presence save a sacramental and spiritual one.

They were heretics, he said, who affirmed that the sacrament gave all the appearance of being bread but was not. Why did they propagate such errors? Why? Because, like the priests of Baal, they wanted to offer their Masses for sale. He closed with the words, "With whom, think you, you are contending? With an old man on the brink of the grave? No, with truth. Truth which is stronger than you and will overcome you." With these words he turned to leave, and his enemies felt paralysed. "Like his divine Master at Nazareth", says d'Aubigne, "he passed through the midst of them."

Leaving Oxford he went back to his parish at Lutterworth. He was never permitted to return to his beloved Oxford, but his greatest work was to be done in the remoteness and quietness of Lutterworth. He was out of favour with men yet the hand of God was upon him, and nothing could prevent him from doing the work appointed for him by his Master.

5.

Wycliffe's Bible.

Wycliffe's last two years were spent at the place where he did his greatest work. He had become Rector back in 1374 but could now spend all his time at Lutterworth. Here he was free from the scholastic constraints of the University and was providentially protected from interference. He could firstly: complete his translation of the Bible into English with the assistance of others; secondly: develop, expound fully and publish his theological views; and thirdly: train and send out his preachers. The setting was ideal.

Here at Lutterworth his feet were well and truly on the ground. He was in a local church and did not neglect the needs of the local parishioners. Most of his sermons that are still in print were preached from the pulpit at Lutterworth. He encouraged his preachers, by his own example, to keep their messages within the range of their hearers' understanding. The Oxford don spent his last years as pastor of a local church. At the same time, his activities for the benefit of the country at large were to be more fruitful than at any other period in his life.

The Bible – Forbidden Book

His most important achievement, and that for which he is most remembered, was his translation of the Bible into English. This was completed in 1382. He wasn't the first to set about this task. The Venerable Bede translated John's Gospel into Saxon, but it did not survive. Alfred the Great translated the Ten Commandments. Early in the reign of Edward III two English versions of the Psalms were made by William Schorham and Richard Roll, but few knew about them. All that was available was Jerome's Latin Vulgate.

This was bad enough, but the laity (i.e. not members of the clergy) were not allowed to

The church at Lutterworth

read it. In the early thirteenth century it was decreed, "We forbid the laity to possess any of the books of the Old and New Testaments, except perhaps the Psalter or Breviary for the Offices of the Hours of the Blessed Virgin, which some, out of devotion, wish to have; but having any of these books translated into the vulgar tongue we strictly forbid."

Wycliffe's attitude towards this decree was the same as that which he had towards all the other monstrous impositions of the Roman Church: he despised it and ignored it.

Knighton, a leading historian of the day, and one whose constant complaints about Wycliffe furnish us with a great deal of useful information, not only complains about Wycliffe's work but gives us a clear view of why the Church was opposed to the common people having the Word of God in their own language.

> Christ gave his Gospel to the clergy and learned of the Church that they might give it to the laity and more infirm persons, according to the exigency of the time and the need of the persons. But this Master John Wyclif translated the Gospel from the Latin into the Anglican language not the angelican. And Wyclif, by thus translating the Bible made it the property of the masses and common to all and more open to the laity and even to women who were able to read, than formerly it had been even to the scholarly and most learned of the clergy. And so the Gospel pearl is thrown before swine and trodden underfoot, and that which used to be so dear to both clergy and laity has become a joke, and this precious gem of the clergy has been turned into the sport of the laity, so that what used to be the highest gift of the clergy and the learned members of the Church has become common to the laity.

Archbishop Arundel said similar things:

> This pestilential and most wretched John Wycliffe of damnable memory, a child of the old devil, and himself a child or pupil of Anti-Christ, who, while he lived, walking in the vanity of his mind . . . [with a few other adjectives, adverbs and verbs, which I shall not give], crowned his wickedness by translating the Scriptures into the mother tongue.

In 1408 he presided at the Council which decreed,

> That no one henceforth translate any text of Holy Scripture into the English tongue, or any other, nor let any such book now lately composed in the time of John Wycliffe be read in whole or in part, in public or in private, under the pain of the greater excommunication till the said translation shall be approved either by the Bishop of the Diocese.

This virtually prohibited its translation.

Wycliffe was not one to take such words lying down.

> **You say it is heresy to speak of the Holy Scriptures in English. You call me a heretic because I have translated the Bible into the common tongue of the people. Do you know whom you blaspheme? Did not the Holy Ghost give the Word of God at first in the mother-tongue of the nations to whom it was addressed? Why do you speak**

Wycliffe's Bible at Hereford Cathedral

against the Holy Ghost? You say that the Church of God is in danger from this book. How can that be? Is it not from the Bible only that we learn that God has set up such a society as a Church on the earth? Is it not the Bible that gives all her authority to the Church? Is it not from the Bible that we learn who is the Builder and Sovereign of the Church, what are the laws by which she is to be governed, and the rights and privileges of her members?

Without the Bible, what charter has the Church to show for all these? It is you who place the Church in jeopardy by hiding the Divine warrant, the missive royal of her King, for the authority she wields and the faith she enjoins.

Lollards were to be condemned not only for reading the Bible but for even hearing it read. For Wycliffe translating the Bible was a task which simply *had* to be accomplished in spite of the prohibition. Men must be able to read for themselves the Word of God. He believed he was handling the very oracles of God, and every part was to be accepted without reserve.

Wycliffe's Attitude

He declared plainly:

Christ and his Apostles taught the people in the language best known to them. It is certain that the truth of the Christian faith becomes more evident the more the faith itself is known. Therefore, the doctrine should not only be in Latin but in the common tongue, and as the faith of the Church is contained in the Scriptures, the more these are known in a true sense the better. The laity ought to understand the faith, and as the doctrines of our faith are in the Scriptures, believers should have the Scriptures in a language familiar to the people, and to

this end indeed did the Holy Spirit endue them with the knowledge of all tongues. If it is heresy to read the Bible, then the Holy Ghost himself is condemned who gave in tongues to the Apostles of Christ to speak the Word of God in all languages that were ordained of God under heaven. If Christ was so merciful as to send the Holy Ghost to the heathen men to make them partakers of his blessed word, why should it be taken from us in this land that be Christian men? If you deny Christ's words as heresy, then you make Christ a heretic. If you condemn the Word of God in any language as heresy, then you condemn God for a heretic that spake the word, for he and his word are all one: and if his word is the life of the world how may any Anti-Christ take it away from us that are Christian men, and allow the people to die for hunger in heresy.

His Bible

Much has been written of a technical nature about the Wycliffe Bible, and opinions vary with regard to the part he played in its production. It is certain, however, that the man who loved the Word so dearly, and was an expert in Latin and theology, would be primarily responsible for this great work. It is considered that he was responsible for the whole of the New Testament, but that Dr. Nicholas de Hereford of Oxford and John Purvey, Wycliffe's assistant at Lutterworth, translated the Old, which was supervised and partly revised by Wycliffe. His translation was very literal and not long after his death Purvey revised it.

His translation marked an epoch in the development of the English language, as Luther's did in the history of the German language. Chaucer has been recognised as the father of English poetry but many consider that Wycliffe should be recognised as the father of English prose. He wrote about 160 works, (65 in English and 96 in Latin) but his translation of the Bible seemed to be on a higher plane. He was evidently stimulated by the knowledge that he was dealing with the Word of God. He believed the very words were inspired, and would doubtless have taken enormous care as a result.

Inspiration of the Text

Stacey tells us that Wycliffe was a contender for "what is now called Fundamentalism". Trevelyan tells us, "We find exactly the same devotion to the literal text in Wycliffe and his followers as among the later Puritans." Wycliffe asserted, "It is impossible for any part of the Holy Scriptures to be wrong. In Holy Scripture is all the truth; one part of Scripture explains another."

It appears that he attempted to improve upon the text of the earlier editions of the Vulgate. He has been criticised for what appear to be deviations from the text but, in many cases, the Latin stood in need of correction and Wycliffe was considerably nearer the truth. Some of his expressions are familiar to readers of the Authorized Version. "Compass sea and land, firstfruits, strait gate, son of perdition, enter thou into the joy of thy Lord." John 7:14-18 and John 14 are almost identical in the Authorized Version. Nevertheless, his translation inevitably exhibits some of the erroneous readings of the Vulgate.

It must have given Wycliffe great joy to complete this enormous task. According to Stacey, he was called 'The Evangelical Doctor', because of his love for the Bible and his constant references to it. The task of translating was great, but the task of publishing was in some ways even greater. Printing was not yet invented. That meant that every copy had to be hand-written. There must have been hundreds of busy hands at work in view of the fact that there are still extant, after 600 years, about 170 hand-written versions of Wycliffe's Bible. Most of them were written after Archbishop Arundel's prohibition.

There were a great number who worked hard copying the Bible, but many more who wanted to buy it. Some ordered whole copies, others were content with portions. Only the wealthiest could afford the whole Bible. The King and royal princes are said to have had copies of Wycliffe's Bible, and all classes obtained them. Bearing in mind the attempts to suppress his Bible, and to destroy them as soon as they were found, the fact that so many are still with us gives us some indication of the enormous number that must have been produced.

The famous painting by Yeames on the cover of this book depicts Wycliffe's preachers going out with books under their arms. These were doubtless portions of the Word of God. It has been estimated that it would cost a man six months' wages to pay for a New Testament. A farmer gave a load of hay for a portion containing a few chapters. A small selection of passages from Wycliffe's Bible will be of interest to the reader.

How wonderful it must have been for these men and women when they read for the first time the story of creation:

In the firste made God of nougt heuene and erthe. The erthe forsothe was veyn with ynne and void, and derknessis weren vpon the face of the see; and the Spiryt of God was born vpon the watrys. And God seide, Be maad ligt; and maad is ligt. And God sawg ligt, that it was good, and deuydid [divided] ligt fro derknessis; and clepide [called] ligt, day and derknessis, nygt. And maad is euen

and moru [morn], o day.

Seide forsothe God, Be maad a firmament in the myddel of watres, and dyuyde it watres from watrys. And God made the firmament, and dyuydid watris that weren undre the firmament from thes that weren aboue the firmament; and it is maad so. And God clepide the firmament, heuene. And maad is euen and moru, the seconde day.

Or consider how their hearts would be filled with thankfulness when they read from Psalm 103:

Blesse thou, my soule, to the Lord; and alle thingus that withinne me ben, to his holi name. Blesse thou, my soule, to the Lord; and wile thou not forgete all the geldingus of hym. That hath mercy to alle thi wickidnessis; that helith alle thin infirmytees. That ageen bieth fro deth thi lif; that crouneth thee in mercy and mercy doingis. That fulfilleth in goode thingus the diseyr; shal be renewid as of an egle thi youthe. Aftir oure synnes he dide not to vs; ne aftir oure wickidnessis he gelde to vs. For after the heigte of heuene fro erthe; he strengthide his mercy vpon men dredende hym.

How moved they must have been to read Isaiah 53:3-8:

And wee desireden hym, dispisid, and the laste of men, man of sorewes, and witenede infirmyte. And as hid his chere and dispisid, wherefore ne wee setteden by him. Vereli oure sicnesses he tooc, and oure sorewes he bar; and wee heelden hym as leprous, and smyten of God, and mekid. He forsothe woundid is for oure wickidnesses, defoulid is for oure hidous giltes; the discyplyne of our pes vp on hym, and with his wannesse we ben heled. Alle wee as shep erreden, eche in to his weie bowede doun, and the Lord putte in hym the wickidness of vs alle. He is offred, for he wolde, and he openede not his mouth; as a shep to sleyng he shal be lad, and as a lomb bifor the clippere itself he shal become doumb, and he opened not his mouth.

What comfort to those who felt their sin when they read Matthew 11:28-30:
Alle ye that traueilen, and ben chargid, come to me, and I shal refreshe, or fulfille you. Take ye my yok on you, and lerne ye of me, for I am mylde and meke in herte; and ye schulen fynde reste to youre soulis. For my yok is softe, and my charge ligt [i.e. burden or load is light].

Or that well-known verse in John 3:16:
Forsothe God so louede the world, that he gaf his oon bigetun sone, that ech man that bileueth in to him perische not, but haue euerlastinge lyf.

And John 6:35-7:
I am the breed of lyf; he that cometh to me, schal not hungre; he that bileueth in me, schal neuere thirste.

Passing on to the Epistles, the profound dignity of Paul's words ring forth:
Who therefore schal departe vs from the charite of God? tribulacioun, or angwisch, or hungur, or nakidness, or persecucioun, or perel, or swerd? As it is writun, For we ben slayn al day for thee; We ben gessid as scheep to slaugtir. But in alle thes thingis we ouercomen, for him that lovede vs. Sothli [truly] I am certeyn, for nether deeth, nether lyf, nether angels, nether pryncipatis, nether virtutes, nether potestatis, nether present thingis, nether thingis to comynge, nether strengthe, nether higthe, nether depnesse, nether othir creature schal may departe us fro the charite of God, that is in Jhesu Crist oure Lord. (Romans 8:35-39)

Finally John's vision as set forth in Revelation 21:1-4:
And I saw newe heuen and newe erthe; forsothe the first heuen and the firste erthe wenten awey, and now is not the se. And I Joon saw the holy citee Jerusalem, newe, comynge doun fro heuen of God, maad redy as a wijf ourned [adorned] to hir husbonde. And

I herde a greet voys of the trone, seiynge,
Lo! the tabernacle of God with men, and
he shal dwelle with hem; and thei shulen
be his puple, and he God with hem shal
be her God. And God shal wijpe awey
eche teer fro the eyen of hem; and deeth
shal no more be, nether moornyng,
nether criyng, nether sorowe shal be
ouer; the whiche firste thinges wenten
awey.

Burrows pays this tribute to Wycliffe's
translation: "It is now a commonplace to
recognise Wycliffe's translation of the English
Bible to the nation as an era in the English
language. It is not Chaucer to whom is
assigned a solitary place of grandeur in the
establishment of the English which we now
speak." Tennyson also honours Wycliffe's
Bible in his poem 'Sir John Oldcastle, Lord
Cobham', who was the most outstanding
Lollard martyr:

Not least art thou, thou little Bethlehem
In Judah, for in thee the Lord was born;
Nor thou in Britain, little Lutterworth,
Least, for in thee the word was born
    again.
Heaven-sweet Evangel, ever-living word,
Who whilome spakest to the South in
    Greek
About the soft Mediterranean shores,
And then in Latin to the Latin crowd,
As good need was – thou hast come to talk
    our isle.
Hereafter thou, fulfilling Pentecost,
Must learn to use the tongues of all the
    world.
Yet art thou thine own witness that thou
    bringest
Not peace, a sword, a fire.

Lutterworth in Leicestershire has the great
honour of being the place where the English
received the first Bible they could read in their
own language.

6.

Wycliffe's 'Bible-Men'.

The last years of his life were the best, though his health could not have been very good when he retired to Lutterworth, banished from the University. It is thought that the illness referred to earlier, which nearly brought about his death, was caused by his intense labour and the ceaseless harassing persecutions, coupled with the fact that he did not appear to have a strong constitution.

Portraits of him, while varying considerably, all represent him as a man of meagre physical strength – unlike Luther. It seems that he never fully recovered from the sickness that he succumbed to when the friars hoped for a recantation before an early death. He had not long to live, but spent all his remaining strength on his crowning achievements. We have already referred to his Bible. Later we shall refer to his theological understanding which was getting clearer and clearer, but for the moment we shall deal with his preachers.

His 'Bible-Men'

There is some doubt as to precisely when Wycliffe began to send out his 'Bible-Men', but Lechler is confident: "I have not a moment's doubt that while he was still at Oxford, Wycliffe sent out his voluntary itinerant preachers, young men belonging to this circle of devoted students who had attached themselves closely to his person and had embraced his theological views as well as his practical principles."

It is important to remember that these students would not be laymen. Even after his expulsion from Oxford this was still true. The majority of his preachers, though not having a scholastic training, were nevertheless still clerks of the church. Wycliffe's 'Bible-Men', while they were unauthorised preachers (i.e. without benefices and lacking a bishop's licence), were still priests of the church. They were known as 'Poor Priests', and had once been ordained. Wycliffe's enemies would have raised a great outcry if this had not been the case.

It must be said, however, that Wycliffe gave a greater place to laymen than did Luther, and that he considered every true Christian as a 'priest' in the New Testament sense, and came eventually to the opinion that they could administer the Lord's Supper and Baptism (the only two 'sacraments' he recognised).

Their Success

He was anxious that they should move about and not settle. They were to avoid frequenting hunting and taverns, but to give themselves to the serious study and preaching of the Word of God. They soon covered the land. Their enemies complained, "They went all over England, seducing nobles and great lords. Their number very much increased and that, starting like saplings from the root of the tree, they were multiplied and filled every place within the compass of the land, to bring over to their sect a great number of the people." Their influence was so great that Wycliffe reckoned that one third of the priests agreed with him on the Lord's Supper, not believing in transubstantiation.

Diocesan records relating to the later persecution of the Lollards are found throughout most of the country. Knighton complained of the 'Bible-Men' that, "Like their master they were too eloquent; that, mighty in words, they exceeded all men in making speeches." and, "Both men and women though even recently converted to this sect were distinguished by some modes of speech and wonderful agreement to the same opinions." He complained, "every second man you met was a Lollard". However, there were many who, while hating the Church, did not love the Bible.

The friars were bitter enemies of these 'Bible-Men'. This did not worry Wycliffe. He urged his men to, **"Preach openly to the people that God counteth more by works of mercy which be in a man's soul than by offerings given to friars, and thou shalt have enemies anon to condemn thee of heresy."**

Persecution

Everything was done to try to stamp out these preachers. The friars, the parish priests and the bishops were united in their opposition. The law of the land was used to try to suppress them. Wycliffe prayed that **"God, in his grace, will raise up for the king from his ministers those who will show up the folly of this law and procedure".**

Wycliffe would not be put off.

Worldly prelates command that no man should preach the Gospel but according to their will and limitation, and forbid men to hear the Gospel on pain of the great curse, but Satan in his own person does never do so much despite to Christ and to his Gospel, for he quoted Holy Writ in tempting Christ and thereby would have pursued his intent, and since it is the counsel and commandment of Christ to priests generally that they preach the Gospel, and as this they must not do without leave of prelates, who it may be are fiends of hell, it follows that priests may not do the commands of Christ without the leave of fiends.

He breaks into prayer:

Ah, Lord Jesus, are these sinful fools, and in some cases fiends of hell, more witty and mighty than thou, that true men may not do thy will without authority from them?

He continues:

Ah, Lord God Almighty, all wise and all full of love, how long wilt thou suffer these Anti-Christs to despise thee and thy holy Gospel, and prevent the health of souls of christian men? Lord of endless righteousness, this thou sufferest, because of sin generally reigning among the people; but of thine endless mercy and goodness, help thy poor wretched priests and servants, that they possess the love and reverence of thy gospel, and be not hindered to do thy worship and will by the false feignings of Anti-Christ.

Methods of 'Lollard' Preachers

Many ideas have been propounded to explain the derivation of the name 'Lollard' that was given to Wycliffe's 'Bible-Men'. Some think it means 'a tare', and certainly their enemies would consider them as tares being sown among the wheat. Others consider the word comes from the German 'lollen' – to sing with a low voice. They were remarkable for their devotional singing, and were obliged to meet in caves and woods where their singing would certainly not be loud so as not to give away their whereabouts.

Preaching, however, was central to their worship, and Wycliffe had a great deal to say against the elaborate singing that was coming into the churches in his day. His preachers were easily recognised. They wore no shoes, had a staff in their hand, and were clothed in a long, russet-coloured gown reaching down to their heels, with deep pockets. They would also carry portions of Wycliffe's Bible.

Misrepresented

Their enemies described them as being subversive. The Peasants' Revolt in 1381 set

Wayside preaching

back Wycliffe's cause considerably, not because he was responsible for it in any way but because it was used to frighten many in the country. It is true that he had far more sympathy with the peasants than did Luther, and that he taught men to think for themselves. And this they did. John Ball, a priest and one of the leaders of the revolt, was responsible for the famous saying, "When Adam delved and Eve span, who then was the gentleman?" But Wycliffe and John Ball had little in common. Wycliffe's preachers showed no hostility to the landowners; in fact, they cultivated the friendship of the landed gentry and were often welcomed to the manor house. This patronage was a great help, and frequently their patrons' support secured them a good hearing. The lord of the manor would even provide an armed guard to ensure their safety while preaching.

Walsingham, who hated Wycliffe, says that "lords and the highest men in the land supported them in their preaching, and favoured those who taught erroneous conclusions since they assigned such great authority to laymen, even the authority to deprive ecclesiastics of their temporalities". It is interesting that while he attacks their opinions, he does not try to blacken their characters. He is obliged to concede that they were "men of serious deportment, despising wealth, never seen in taverns, never heard to swear, concise and devout in their prayers and preaching charity".

Preaching Everywhere

There was no limit to the places they would choose for preaching. They preached in churches where they were open to them, and where they were closed, in churchyards, on village greens, in public squares or by the fireside, or in other "profane places". Wycliffe found divine precedent for this:

> **Jesus ever had this manner, to speak God's Words where he knew that they might profit the people who heard them, and so Christ preached often, now at meat and now at supper, and at whatever time it was convenient for others to hear him.**

Their success was complained of:

> In this year the friars have been deprived of their alms, the mendicants are compelled to work, they are not allowed to preach – they are called 'penny preachers and creepers into houses'. Besides this the poor preachers write scandalous pamphlets in English and write down their essays likewise in English.

Training of Preachers

At Lutterworth he could concentrate on his task of training and sending out his preachers. He was far more at home doing this from Lutterworth than from Oxford. His concern was with the ability of his disciples to evangelise rather than with their scholarship.

> If divinity were learned on that manner that Apostles did, it should profit much more than it doth now by the manner of study of priests now. Men of scholarship travail vainly for to get new subtleties and the profit of Holy Church by this way is put aback.

He was extremely disappointed by the reception he received at Oxford for his doctrine of the Lord's Supper. The authorities succeeded in preventing his fellow dons from giving him any support. It is not surprising that he should add: "An unlearned man with God's grace does more for the Church than many graduates. Scholastic studies rather breed than destroy heresies."

Wycliffe came to believe that much academic study was useless for a man who wished to enter the Christian ministry. "Let the faithful man discover what knowledge helps most to virtuous life and labour hard to grasp it." Christ's church does not need "learned graduates promoted to fat benefices, but simple men following Christ and his doctrine".

He believed that graduates tended to replace the Scriptures by "poems and fables". It would be no loss for men to set aside academic training because of the perils attached to the title of Master. When he was accused of inconsistency because of his own academic training, he accepted it, "humbly confessing his past sins and seeking to warn others lest they fall into the same danger".

Men must be familiar with the Word of God above everything else. He believed that by preaching "They sow the seed of the Word of Christ more humbly and more abundantly both in work and in word." Increasingly the Lollard preachers came from the lower ranks of society, and these more than replaced those who were deserting his cause. Wycliffe himself set an example in his preaching. He considered it to be more important than any other function of the pastoral office, and to be the principal means of grace.

7.

Wycliffe the Preacher.

Wycliffe preached a great deal himself and was considered to be the greatest preacher of his day. He preached occasionally in London, as well as at Oxford, to great effect. Indeed, it was his very preaching in the churches of London which first stirred the bishops to take public action against him. It was bad enough to have him teaching his 'heresies' at Oxford, and advising king and parliament, but when he reached the ears of the masses they were thoroughly alarmed.

Wycliffe, in his preaching as in all else, based everything on the Word of God. This is in marked contrast to what the people were used to. It is important for us to realise that in his day the people regularly heard popular preaching, but not serious exposition of the Scriptures. It would be wrong for us to imagine that the sending out of his preachers was a novelty. There was nothing new about it at all. What was new was the **content** and **method** of their preaching.

Evangelism by Entertainment

The people were thoroughly familiar with preaching – or perhaps we should say 'religious entertainment'. It was common for all kinds of people to move about from place to place, whether they were minstrels, pedlars, actors, acrobats or penny preachers. The friars filled their sermons with legends of saints, insipid stories, tragedies, fables, coarse buffooneries, unwholesome illustrations and interpretations of dreams. No tale was deemed too preposterous if it would hold the people's attention. "The multitude were amused, the collection was good, the sale of indulgences satisfactory and the penny preacher could go on his way

Preaching at St Paul's Cross

rejoicing, for there were friars of whom it was said that they would preach more for a bushel of wheat than to bring a soul out of hell."

The Dominicans and the Franciscans were specially trained for the work of popular preaching and they humoured the corrupt taste of the time. Allegorical interpretations and applications came into general use and helped men to avoid putting Scripture into practice (by avoiding the simple meaning of the text).

Carrick, in his 'Wycliffe and the Lollards',

devotes a chapter to Wycliffe's poor preachers. He describes the preaching of the friars as "not the declaration of the truths and doctrines of the faith, but general harangues on whatever took their fancy, and their great aim was to attract the attention and sustain the interest of their hearers by any means".

Use of Drama

The Church used the spectacular display of sacred themes very widely. It appeared to them that drama was not only harmless but had an almost infinite power for good. Prior to the Reformation the mystery plays were performed more widely in England than anywhere else. According to Carrick, "The Reformers were at a loss how to regard these highly popular methods of amusing and instructing the people." Wycliffe vigorously and consistently denounced these exhibitions and representations of Bible scenes and people, while Luther declared that "such spectacles often did more good and produced more impression than sermons".

Wycliffe's view was that the pictorial and spectacular teaching of the church should be superseded by the simple preaching of the simple Gospel, and that an *end* should be made of theatrical instruction. What was novel about Wycliffe was that he believed that the preacher should dispense with *everything but the scripture*.

Friar preaching

Elaborate Singing

Another feature that was prominent in Wycliffe's day, was what he describes as "the novelry of song". Singing had become very elaborate, with a kind of trilling, described as "knacking". He also uses the expression "tattering", which appears to have been the cutting up of the Scriptures into shreds for performance by singers.

Wycliffe also complained that this religious entertainment not only diverted the attention from true devotion but was maintained at enormous cost that could be better used.

These performances were frivolous, "it stirred vain men to dancing more than mourning", and he warns "fools" who find pleasure in it that they "should dread the sharp words of Augustine that says 'as oft as the song delights me more than that which is sung, so oft I confess that I sin grievously'".

As for the argument that the Temple services of the Old Testament could be imitated, he rejected them as models for Christian worship, which should be distinguished by simplicity and spirituality,

and if they say that angels serve God by song in heaven, we say that we know not that song: they be in full victory of their enemies; but we be in perilous battle, and in the valley of weeping and mourning; and our song hindereth [such song would hinder] us from better occupation, and stirreth us to many great sins, and to forget ourselves. But our fleshly people hath more liking in their bodily ears, in such knacking [trilling] and tattering [tearing up into shreds], than in hearing of God's law, or speaking of bliss of heaven.

When they be forty or fifty in a choir, three or four proud rogues shall knack the most devout service, when no man shall hear the sentence, and all other shall be dumb, and look on them, as fools. And thus the true service of God is hindered and this vain knacking, for our jollity and pride, is praised above the moon.

It should be pointed out that instrumental music had just been introduced into divine service. When the Lollard William Thorpe was later examined, the Archbishop said that "organs and good delectable songs quickened and sharpened men's wits more than should any sermon". This attitude angered Wycliffe more than almost anything else. "Christ did not teach his disciples to sing but to preach the gospel."

To Wycliffe the Word of God had to be central. It was neglected even in preaching itself. He strongly censured those who were guilty of "not preaching God's Word". We must not assume that sermons of the kind he condemned were not preached from some Bible text. What happened was rather that the preachers, *after giving out* a text from the Scriptures, took the *main contents* of their sermon from *other* sources.

Exposition of Scripture

Wycliffe's great concern was for true '*Biblical exposition*'. He not only objected to the neglect of the Word, but the wrong preaching of the Word when a *proper* attempt was made. The language of the Word of God was thrust into the background, and the language of the *preacher* alone came to the fore. It was as if he *himself* were the author and discoverer of God's truth. "This practise", remarks Wycliffe, "comes from nothing else but the pride of man; everyone seeking his own honour, everyone preaching only himself and not Jesus Christ."

In Wycliffe's sermons we have an *opening up* of the text and demonstration and *proving* of the interpretation of it, such as we find not only in the Apostle Paul in his preaching in the synagogues, but in a typical Puritan sermon. For him it was not enough for the preacher to assert his views, to say what he thought was right, he had to prove it from the Scriptures: Wycliffe wanted the Scriptures to interpret themselves.

Wycliffe blames a failure to expound the Scriptures as the reason for the prevailing spiritual deadness. "It is a dead word, not the Word of our Lord Jesus Christ, not the Word of eternal life." For Wycliffe, the Word of God was the indispensable Bread of Life, the seed of regeneration and conversion.

Repeatedly Wycliffe insisted that the Scripture must be interpreted in a manner consistent with its general sense. He warns against those who are guilty of "tearing the Scriptures in pieces". The whole of Holy Scripture was the one Word of God. It was in harmony with itself.

Preaching Method

He began by taking the literal sense of the Scriptures and would not allow a man to *invent* a figurative sense at *his pleasure*. His aim was to arrive at a *spiritual sense* of the text which was couched in the *simple* sense of the words. He knew how to make Scripture passages yield a sense as *simple* as it was full and rich. For instance, the prevailing interpretation of Luke 22:38, "See here are two swords", with the answer of the Lord Jesus, "It is enough", was that this was a Scriptural proof of the dogma that Peter had been given a two-fold power signified by the two swords. Wycliffe objected to such a leap from the literal sense to the spiritual sense *if this figurative meaning was not founded upon other passages of scripture*. It is important to look closely at Wycliffe's approach, since he was the model for the Lollard preachers.

There were three methods of preaching in Wycliffe's day. One was called 'declaring', in which the preacher took a subject or text and delivered what was more an oration or essay on it, than a sermon. The second was to take a text and divide it, and sub-divide it: a method which continued many years after Wycliffe's day. Some seventeenth century sermons were described as 'branching' sermons because they could have a dozen points at least. The Scripture had recently been divided into its present order of chapters, and the schoolmen loved to divide and sub-divide, and that was their manner. The third method was to 'postillate', which was to commence with reading a portion of

Scripture and then to explain it. This latter method was the one adopted by Wycliffe, which was a form of exposition of Scripture. However the sermons we have included in the final chapter were more topical and mostly from a volume of small tracts.

Evangelistic Fervour

Wycliffe's sermons were full of Bible truth, and so were those of his preachers. Though he was an academic, he could plead with men from the heart:

> Lift up, wretches, the eyes of your soul and behold him that no spot of sin was in, what pain he suffered for sin of man. He swat water and blood to wash thee of sin; he was bound and beaten with scourges, the blood running adown by his sides, that thou shouldest keep thy body clean in his service; he was crowned with sharp thorns that thou shouldest think of him and flee all cursed malice; he was nailed to the cross with sharp nails through hands and feet and stung to the heart with a sharp spear that all thy five wits should be ruled after him, having mind on the five precious wounds that he suffered for man.

> And right in all his great pain this Innocent prayed for his enemies to his Father and said: 'Father forgive them this guilt for they know not what they do.'

His evangelistic zeal could not be doubted by those who have read his works:

> Just as Moses hoisted the adder in the desert to heal the people by looking on him, so must mannis sone [the Son of Man], be hoisted up upon the cross. Christ was in the form of the adder of venom but he had no venom in him. But as right looking on this adder of brass saved the people from the venom of the serpent, so right looking by full belief in Christ saved his people from sin.

Confidence in Scripture

He had great confidence in the effectiveness of the Word of God:

> Some men tell tales that they find in the saints' lives outside Holy Scriptures. And such thing often pleaseth more the people. But we hold this manner good – to leave such words and trust in God and tell surely his law and specially his Gospels. And, since these words are God's words, they should be taken as believed, and they will quicken men, give them life, new life, more than other words.

This confidence comes out particularly in a wonderful passage which shows us his heart, when he cries out:

> O marvellous power of the Divine Seed! which overpowers strong men in arms,

softens hard hearts, and renews and changes into divine men, men who had been brutalized by sins, and departed infinitely far from God. Obviously such miraculous power could never be worked by the word of a priest, if the Spirit of Life and the Eternal Word did not, above all things else, work with it.

He has been criticised for lack of evangelistic zeal for the souls of men, but these quotations speak for themselves.

The distinguishing mark of Wycliffe's poor preachers was their sermons. Their sermons were more of an ethical than of a dogmatic character. Their chief duty was "faithfully to scatter the seed of God's Word, and to expose the gross open sins prevailing in different ranks, and the hypocrisy and error of the teaching of Anti-Christ and his followers".

Simplicity in Preaching

It must have been a great temptation to Wycliffe to seek satisfaction in a scholarly handling of the Scriptures. Lechler's words are invaluable in giving us a clear picture of Wycliffe the preacher:

All his thinking, every intellectual achievement, was always a way to an end, a means of moral action and work, it never terminated in itself. At no time was it his aim to give his addresses, sermons, etc., an artistic shape, to polish them, to bring them to a certain perfection of form, but to promote the glory of God, the Kingdom of Christ, and the salvation of souls.

If only what he said was *understood*, if his written word was only *effective* and his action was only valued by any *good fruit*, then it troubled him little that his style was thought to be without finish or without beauty, or perhaps even wearisome. Wycliffe always communicates *himself*; his whole personality, undissembled, true and full, as a preacher as well as a writer; he is always the *whole* man. In him the intellect predominated, but it was harmoniously combined with a powerful and heroic will.

But we are not to imagine he was devoid of feeling.

He shows a moral indignation and horror in the very midst of a learned investigation where one is not at all prepared for such an outburst of flaming feeling. At other times, in the very middle of a disputation with opponents, he breaks out into joyful thanksgiving and praise to God that he has been set free from the errors by which they are still held fast. Together with this there was an absolute and perfect integrity and unreserved sincerity.

He never concealed the **changes** of opinion through which he passed, ***openly*** confessing when he had previously done homage to error. He grew holy himself with the holy aims which he pursued. His personal character was exalted by the cause which he served, and the cause which he served was never truth as mere knowledge but as a power unto godliness.

Instruction to his Preachers

At Lutterworth, Wycliffe gave both examples of how to preach and specific instruction. He produced volumes of sermons in English and has left us with a clear understanding of what advice he gave his preachers:

It is irrelevant for the priest to have secular lordship or temporal goods on a permanent basis for the carrying out of his office. Curates should live solely on the material alms of their subjects. By means of preaching Christ creates for himself heirs of the Heavenly Kingdom, even while here on earth. It is not *you* who preach, but the Spirit of the Father which speaks in you and since the works of the Trinity are inseparable, it is the Trinity which speaks.

To the people the Gospel must be preached as God commands. The truth must be proclaimed to them even though they receive it unwillingly. Not comedies or tragedies, not fables or droll stories, but simply and solely the Law of the Lord as Christ and the Apostles delivered it: for in the Law, that is the Gospel, is hidden the life which is able to quicken the church. The Lord's Word is the food which sustains it. He who preaches to the people without reading and explaining to them the Gospel, gives them a meal without bread. Those pseudo prelates set aside the Gospel. If they mention the Gospel at all, they do not preach it in full.

Christ has said, Go out and proclaim that the Kingdom of Heaven is at hand. One must preach of the Kingdom of Heaven, of the Kingdom of Christ, of the Lord's Advent ... but above all, of Christ and his incarnation and of the preparation of man for eternal blessedness. As the time is already at hand in which Christ prepares man for obtaining this blessedness, the preacher must exhort his hearers *to set to work* in order to *obtain* it. [Italics mine in this and the following quotes.]

He insisted that they should adapt their subjects to the comprehension of the hearers.

The sermon should be short but ***complete*** and told in a ***right spirit***.

> If the soul does not harmonise with the words, how can the words have power.
> If love is wanting in thee, thou art sounding brass and a tinkling symbal.
> The sermon should be pointed but not bitter.

His sermons are plain, simple, and include vivid comparisons taken from life.

> He must not trouble himself about *new fashions* in preaching which may arise.
> The only care must be how to be *useful* as far as possible to the people.

Wycliffe divided his sermons into ***two*** sections. In the first he usually dealt with the ***meaning*** of the Biblical passage on which the sermon is based. In the second he set forth the ***doctrine*** with its ***moral application*** addressed to the congregation.

When we appreciate the popular preaching of Wycliffe's day we can value Wycliffe as a preacher and as a trainer of preachers. The communicators of his day would resort to anything in order to secure the interest of their hearers. With these methods Wycliffe, "Puritan in this as in everything else, would have nothing to do. They seemed to him lying and ludicrous, a detraction from the dignity and effectiveness of the message." When we remember how illiterate the people were in his day, and how little they had to read, it is remarkable that Wycliffe should simply rely on the word ***preached***. His 'Bible-Men' "studied the compilation of sermons", writes a hostile chronicler. In Chaucer's 'Poor Parson of the Town', we read that "Cristes Gospel gladly would he preche".

We come to the heart of the man with a quotation on preaching, during which he breaks out into prayer. Here we see not only his heart, but the reason for his usefulness.

> Many men preach themselves and cease from preaching Christ. This ornamental style is little in keeping with God's Word. The latter is rather corrupted by it and its power paralyzed for the conversion and regeneration of souls. God's Word, according to Augustine, has a peculiar and incomparable eloquence of its own, in its very simplicity and modesty of form. A flowery, captivating style of address is of little value compared to right substance. Christ promised to his disciples that it should be given to them *what* they ought to say. The *how* would follow.
>
> Worldly prelates command that no man should preach the gospel except according to their own will and limitation, and forbid men to hear the gospel on pain of the great curse, but since it is the counsel and commandment of Christ to priests generally that they preach the gospel,

and as this they must do without leave
of prelates, who it may be are fiends of
hell, it follows that priests may do the
commands of Christ without the leave
of fiends.

The Holy Spirit

He was conscious of the great need of the
Holy Spirit to give success to the preacher,
especially bearing in mind the opposition he
faced. His prayer showed his sense of
dependence upon the Holy Spirit in the work
of the ministry.

Almighty Lord God, most merciful, and
in wisdom boundless, since thou
sufferedst Peter and all apostles to
have so great fear and cowardice at the
time of thy passion, that they flew all
away for dread of death, and for a poor
woman's voice; and since afterwards,
by the comfort of the Holy Ghost, thou
madest them so strong that they were
afraid of no man, nor of pain, nor death;
help now, by gifts of the same Spirit, thy
poor servants, who all their life have
been cowards, and make them strong,
and bold in thy cause, to maintain the
gospel against Anti-Christ, and the
tyrants of this world.

Chaucer's Poor Parson

We shall conclude this chapter with

The Poor Parson (Canterbury Tales)

Chaucer's description of the 'Poor Parson'.
We do not know at what point Wycliffe and
Chaucer made contact, or precisely what
relationship they had, but we can be confident
that Chaucer held him in high esteem and
that, when describing his 'Poor Parson' in his
Prologue to the 'Canterbury Tales', he had
Wycliffe in mind. There are clear indications
that there was a connection but the
description speaks for itself. Wycliffe's 'Bible-
Men' were, in fact, 'Poor Parsons' or priests.

It is sometimes pointed out that the
Lollards objected to pilgrimages and so could
hardly be portrayed as taking part in one.

However a clear indication of who Chaucer had in mind does emerge. When the 'Poor Parson' reproved the host for swearing the latter exclaims, "I smell a Lollard in the wind." (The Lollards particularly objected to oaths of any kind.) If Chaucer wanted a truly representative company he had to include a Lollard!

Lechler tells us, "There are several features of this portrait which agree with the character of Wycliffe, and not a single trait can be detected in it which does not suit him. The humility, the contentment, and the unselfishness; the moral spotlessness, the compassionate love, the conscientious and diligent faithfulness in his office, and the Biblical character of his preaching – these were all his." When we remember that Chaucer did not share Wycliffe's faith, and was bitterly critical of clerics, his testimony is all the more remarkable.

A good man was ther of religioun
And was a poure ***persoun*** of a toun
But riche he was of holy thoght and
   werk.
He was also a lerned man, a clerk

That Cristes gospel trewely wolde
   preche:
His parisshens devoutly wolde he teche.
Benygne he was and wonder diligent
And in adversitee ful pacient . . .
Wyd was his parisshe and houses fer
   asonder,
But he ne left nat for reyn ne thonder,
In siknesse nor in meschief to visite
The ferreste [furthest] in his parisshe,
   muche and lite [rich and poor],
Upon his feet, and in his hand a staf.
This noble ensample to his sheep he yaf
   [gave]
That first he wroghte and afterward he
   taughte;
Out of the gospel he those wordes
   caughte [took],
And this figure he added eek [also]
   therto
That if gold ruste, what shal iren do?
For if a preest be foul on whom we
   truste,
No wonder is a lewed man to ruste . . .
But Cristes loore and his apostles twelve
He taughte but first he folwed it hym
   selve.

8.

Last Days at Lutterworth.

Wycliffe had retired to Lutterworth, and was doing his greatest work. But his enemies could not leave him in peace. He knew that it would be simply a matter of time before they silenced him, but there was time enough to complete his allotted task. He knew how to delay his enemies and frustrate them in their designs.

Summoned to Rome

The inevitable happened: he was summoned to appear before the Pontiff in Rome. If he had gone then he would never have returned; but there was another providential over-ruling – he suffered his first stroke and so could not go. He told the Pope he was "hindered by God" from going, but this did not stop him from giving the Pope some advice. He wrote in a sarcastic tone:

I am always glad to explain my faith to anyone, and above all to the Bishop of Rome, for I take it for granted that if he be orthodox he will confirm it. If it be erroneous he will correct it. I assume, too, that as Chief Vicar of Christ Upon Earth the Bishop of Rome is of all mortal men most bound to the law of Christ's Gospel ... Now Christ, during his life upon earth, was of all men the poorest, casting from him all worldly authority. I deduce from these premises as a simple counsel of my own that the Pope should surrender all temporal authority to the civil power and advise his clergy to do the same.

Among other things he went on to say that he was prepared to go to the Pope but "Christ has needed me to the contrary, and taught me more obedience to God than to man".

Death

He had little energy left. His body was getting weaker but he was determined to do all he could till the end came. On the last

Sunday of 1384, as he was about to dispense the Lord's Supper, he became paralysed and fell. It was his third stroke. He was taken in a chair out of a side door in the church to the rectory. Two days later, on 31st December, he died in bed.

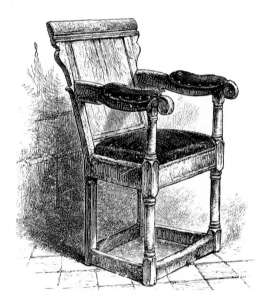

Wycliffe's chair at Lutterworth, which is believed by some to be the one in which he was carried to the rectory after his final stroke.

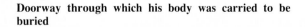

Doorway through which his body was carried to be buried

An inscription on the memorial to him in Lutterworth Parish
Church, dated 1837, reads as follows:

SACRED TO THE MEMORY OF JOHN WICLIF
THE EARLIEST CHAMPION OF ECCLESIASTICAL REFORMATION IN ENGLAND,
HE WAS BORN IN YORKSHIRE IN THE YEAR 1324,
IN THE YEAR 1375 HE WAS PRESENTED TO THE RECTORY OF LUTTERWORTH:
WHERE HE DIED ON THE 31st DECEMBER 1384,
AT OXFORD HE ACQUIRED NOT ONLY THE RENOWN OF A CONSUMMATE SCHOOLMAN,
BUT THE FAR MORE GLORIOUS TITLE OF THE EVANGELIC DOCTOR
HIS WHOLE LIFE WAS ONE IMPETUOUS STRUGGLE AGAINST THE CORRUPTIONS
AND ENCROACHMENTS OF THE PAPAL COURT,
AND THE IMPOSTURES OF ITS DEVOTED AUXILIARIES, THE MENDICANT FRATERNITIES,
HIS LABOURS IN THE CAUSE OF SCRIPTURAL TRUTH
WERE CROWNED BY ONE IMMORTAL ACHIEVEMENT,
HIS TRANSLATION OF THE BIBLE INTO THE ENGLISH TONGUE.
THIS MIGHTY WORK DREW ON HIM, INDEED, THE BITTER HATRED
OF ALL WHO WERE MAKING MERCHANDIZE OF THE POPULAR CREDULITY AND IGNORANCE:
BUT HE FOUND AN ABUNDANT REWARD IN THE BLESSING OF HIS COUNTRYMEN,
OF EVERY RANK AND AGE, TO WHOM HE UNFOLDED THE WORDS OF ETERNAL LIFE.
HIS MORTAL REMAINS WERE INTERRED NEAR THIS SPOT:
BUT THEY WERE NOT ALLOWED TO REST IN PEACE:
AFTER THE LAPSE OF MANY YEARS,
HIS BONES WERE DRAGGED FROM THE GRAVE, AND CONSIGNED TO THE FLAMES:
AND HIS ASHES WERE CAST INTO THE WATERS OF THE ADJOINING STREAM.

(Other records show that John Wycliffe was presented to
Lutterworth in 1374 by Letters Patent, dated 7th April)

Desecration of his Grave

Over thirty years later, on 4th May, 1415, a committee appointed by the Council of Constance in Bavaria to examine Huss and Jerome, also examined Wycliffe's writings, and condemned them as heretical on 260 counts. His influence in Bohemia had been so great that not only were his books burnt, but his bones were ordered to be "dug up and cast out of consecrated ground". Nothing was done until on 9th December, 1427, it was ordered that his body and bones were to be exhumed and publicly burnt, "and his ashes to be disposed of so that no trace of him should be seen again". They were cast into the River Swift at Lutterworth. But Wycliffe was to be heard of a great deal more. The Church of Rome could not silence him.

His Influence

Opinions have varied enormously among Wycliffe's biographers as to the success of all that he sought to achieve. Some have held that he tried to do too much in too short a time, and that if he had been more patient he would have been more successful. One writer goes much farther and accuses him of undermining the very cause he was forwarding, by his forthrightness. The majority of his biographers, nevertheless, have recognised his great contribution to the English Reformation. The great differences that occurred in their estimate of his usefulness depended on their understanding of his goals.

Church and State

It is essential to see that he differed from later Reformers in his methods because of his attitude towards the relationship between Church and State. He did not want support from the State in furthering the Gospel. He relied on the Word of God alone. His remedy for the grievous state of affairs that then existed was twofold. Firstly, the separation from reliance on state support by the Church, and secondly, the free proclamation of the Gospel. He did not have as his objective a State Church run on Protestant lines (as did the Reformers), but liberty and freedom to preach and success in the preaching itself. This was because he relied on the preaching alone to bring success. He failed to achieve that liberty he sought, it is true, but his labours in the evangelistic field were astonishingly successful.

Success

If we are to blame Wycliffe for his boldness in denunciation of error and insistence upon change, we might as well conclude that Stephen, the first martyr, was also too bold in the denunciation he made of the religious authorities of his day. If we condemn Wycliffe

Desecration of Wycliffe's grave

for bringing unnecessary persecution upon his head for "intemperate language", we may as well blame Stephen for the persecution which came upon the Early Church after his outspoken words.

But then there are further parallels. Stephen was wonderfully upheld and strengthened to say what he did. Only Divine strength enabled Wycliffe to pursue his consistent course until he breathed his last breath. Stephen had a glimpse of Heaven before he was taken there; Wycliffe spoke of the "bliss of heaven", and especially of the love of God, in such a way that it is plain he was continually conscious of its nearness. Stephen's words were fulfilled later when the young Saul who heard them, became the Apostle Paul. Wycliffe's evangelistic labours were so successful that he became the Father of the English Reformation.

The Success of Wycliffe's Work

While there has been less interest in Wycliffe in recent years than there has been in the past, a great deal of research has been done on the Lollards. A picture has emerged that has vindicated the words of Fox's later histories. It has become clear that their numbers were far larger than were imagined, and that, far from dying out, they were already increasing when the Reformation came from Germany.

Wycliffe was, above all, a man of faith, not an ecclesiastical politician. He sowed the seed "in hope". He declared boldly and plainly whatever truth he discovered in the Word of God as soon as he discovered it, to whoever would listen, by whatever means he could legitimately use. His great faith comes out in his astonishing prophecy, that was literally fulfilled: **"I anticipate that some of the friars whom God shall be pleased to enlighten will return with all devotion to the original religion of Christ, will freely return to primitive truth, and then build up the church as Paul did before them."** He had confidence that the One who enlightened him would enlighten others.

He did not end his days bitter and frustrated, but confident in the One who had given him the light of truth and boldness to

The River Swift at Lutterworth

declare it, and prayer made his heavenly reward very close to him. He expected to die a martyr's death, and faced it with remarkable courage:

To live and be silent, is with me impossible – the guilt of such treason against the Lord of heaven is more to be dreaded than many deaths. Let the blow, therefore, fall. Enough I know of the men whom I oppose, of the times on which I am thrown, and of the mysterious Providence which relates to our sinful race, to believe that the stroke may ere long descend. But my purpose is unalterable: I wait its coming.

He escaped the blow, but his enemies showed their spite by what they did to his bones. This did not prevent his influence from spreading, but provided Thomas Fuller an opportunity to describe in his quaint way the success of Wycliffe's ministry.

The little river conveyed Wycliffe's remains into the Avon, Avon into the Severn, Severn into the narrow seas, they into the main ocean. And thus the ashes of Wycliffe are the emblem of his doctrine, which now is dispensed all the world over.

His Character

It was not just the words of Wycliffe that impressed people, but that he lived by what he preached. His enemies had difficulty in finding fault with his life. There are some blots in the character of Luther from which Wycliffe was free. He was never in the debt of the politicians and was thoroughly consistent in his behaviour. He was a true pastor, and in some ways, the champion of the poorer classes. This led to him being blamed for the Peasants' Revolt. The only words of criticism that can be given credence come from his own pen:

I do readily impart a sinister, vindictive zeal into my legitimate line of argument. As for imputation of hypocrisy, hatred and rancour under a pretence of holiness, I fear I admit with sorrow that this has happened to me frequently.

He did, indeed, have a tempestuous nature, and a sustained capacity for cutting words; but he was never personal, and always argued his case. The words of the Lollard Thorpe, at his trial in 1407, give us a rare insight into Wycliffe's character. He was of "spare, frail, emaciated frame, in habit of life more innocent", and according to Thorpe, the remarkable hold he had over men was not simply due to his immense learning but in part to his charm, as well as his simple way of life.

It was in his last years that his faith shone the brightest. He was getting weaker all the time because of the work load he took, and because of pressure from his enemies. It has been pointed out that:

During the last two years immediately preceding his death, the Father of the English Reformation is seen deserted by the most powerful of his accredited disciples, oppressed by the strength of the hierarchy and fully anticipating martyrdom. It is at such a forbidding crisis that we find his industry in the cause of reform, and his courage in attempting to promote it, augmented rather than diminished, and such as Luther did not surpass even in the most favourable periods of his history.

We shall conclude with an impressive statement about Wycliffe. Perhaps the greatest tribute to him was the notable public testimony given by the University in 1405. It is so striking that it has been challenged and condemned as a forgery, but its genuineness is evident as it was sealed with the common seal of the University, and the authorities have ***never disclaimed*** its authenticity. It is especially remarkable as it was written 5 years after the infamous statute was passed "for the burning of heretics".

Hereupon it followeth, that the special good will and care which we bare unto John Wickliff, sometime child of this our university, and professor of divinity, moving and stirring our minds, as his manners and conditions required no less, with one mind, voice, and testimony, we do witness, all his conditions and doings throughout his whole life to have been most sincere and commendable; whose honest manners and conditions, profoundness of learning, and most redolent renown and fame, we desire the more earnestly to be notified and known unto all faithful, for that we understand the maturity and ripeness of his conversation, his diligent labours and travels to tend to the praise of God, the help and safeguard of others, and the profit of the church.

Wherefore, we signify unto you that his conversation, even from his youth upward, unto the time of his death, was so praiseworthy and honest, that never at any time was there any note or spot of suspicion noised of him. But in his answering, reading, preaching, and determining, he behaved himself laudably, and as a stout and valiant champion of the faith; vanquishing, by the force of the scriptures, all such, who by their wilful beggary blasphemed and slandered Christ's religion. Neither was this doctor convicted of any heresy, either burned of our prelates after his burial. God forbid that our prelates should have condemned a man of such honesty, for a heretic; who, amongst all the rest of the university, hath written in logic, philosophy, divinity, morality, and the speculative art, without equal. The knowledge of all which and singular things we do desire to testify and deliver forth; to the intent that the fame and renown of the said doctor may be the more evident, and had in reputation, amongst them unto whose hands these present letters testimonial shall come.

In witness whereof, we have caused these our letters testimonial to be sealed with our common seal. Dated at Oxford, in our congregation-house October 1st, 1405.

For Wycliffe it was not enough to write the truth: it had to be lived. Men not only read his writings but saw his life, which was truly "an epistle read and known of all men".

Deo Soli Gloria.

9.

Wycliffe's Beliefs.

Wycliffe is known as the man who gave us the first Bible in English. He is also known as the one who sent out preachers, but at the root of this activity was his discovery and propagation of sound doctrine. He was the first of the English reformers; and the greatest. As has been mentioned previously, 'heresy' had not previously troubled the Roman Church in England. There were those who went before Wycliffe who were truly enlightened by the Spirit and understood the way of salvation, but none who were prepared to attack the Church as an institution. His understanding as a thinker and Reformer gradually developed until, in the end, he saw all the major doctrines of the faith.

He was a man of immense intellectual ability and even his enemies recognised that he did not have an equal, but nevertheless he had a child-like faith in the word of God. This submission of mind to the Scriptures, brought him inevitably into the full light of the truth. While he lacked a complete understanding on some minor points of doctrine, he moved into clearer light with surprising rapidity. In this respect he excels even Luther. Luther had a starting point far in advance of Wycliffe – due to some extent to Wycliffe's own writings – yet at the same time he could not see some things as clearly as Wycliffe did. Certainly Luther made plain the doctrine of justification by faith, and gave it an emphasis that is not found in Wycliffe, but that Wycliffe held this doctrine there is no doubt whatever.

Justification by Faith

Some have doubted whether Wycliffe actually believed in 'Justification by Faith' at all. It is true that he gave a more important place to good works than Luther, but we need to remember that Luther dismissed the letter of James as an "epistle of straw" for its emphasis on good works as the evidence of saving faith. It is certainly true that Wycliffe did not make an explicit and theologically-argued distinction between Justification and Sanctification. If the subject had become controversial it would have been a different matter. There can be no doubt whatever that he believed in Justification by Faith from his own words on the subject:

> Trust wholly in Christ, rely altogether on his suffering; beware of seeking to be justified in any other way than by his righteousness. Faith in our Lord Jesus Christ is sufficient for salvation. There must be atonement made for sin according to the righteousness of God. The person to make this atonement must be God and man.

In his message on 'Christ Stilling the Tempest', he says,

> Some men received him, not to the health of their soul, for they were unstable as water. But other men were stable as land, who held the knowledge that Christ put in them. And by the ground of such faith they went fully the way to Heaven.

A further quotation from the same passage will demonstrate this point:

> Belief faileth when it worketh not well indeed but is idle as in a sleeping man

> ... No kind of virtue was praised more of Christ than was right belief, *for it is the ground of all other*. May God increase our faith! We by sin enfeeble our faith. And Christ sleepeth oft to us, for such sleeping of our sin. For when winds of man's boast maketh us to dread worldly harms, and floods of tribulations come to us, they make us dread and cry on Christ for to have help for failing in our belief. For we should know that no such case might annoy us but for sin. And if troubles come because of our sin, it is just and God's will. Why should we be thus distempered for what is needful to come? Love we God, and do we his will, and dread we no kind of thing but him, for default in our belief maketh us to dread for such things.[Italics mine]

In 'The Promise Made to Abraham' he says,

> If a man believe in Christ, and make a point of this belief, then the promise that God hath made to come into the land of light shall be given by virtue of Christ, to all men that make this the chief matter.

Wycliffe always upheld the incomparable grandeur of the Lord Jesus Christ as the only mediator between God and man and said little about the actual mechanics of faith.

It is also objected that Wycliffe's own view of Assurance did not place enough emphasis on faith. He is surely clear enough when he says:

> Each man should dread more the loss of God's love by sin, than he should dread the loss of any worldly things; for as faith teacheth, loss of God's love were worse. And here may men have a mirror to judge whether they love God.

The messages given in the final chapter should remove any lingering doubts about his belief in justification by faith. Most certainly things are emphasised that we may not be used to. He placed greater stress on ethical behaviour than is customary among Evangelicals, but this can be a healthy correction.

Purgatory

The reader of Wycliffe's works may well be surprised and dismayed by his reference to Purgatory. It is clear that he changed his opinion on the subject, as in so many other matters, through his study of the Scriptures. He changed from referring to the "pains of purgatory", to viewing purgatory as a place where the saints rested. In common with others, he believed that there was an intermediate stage before reaching Heaven, and spoke of "the saints sleeping and resting in purgatory". It was hardly a place to be afraid of!

He frequently referred to the "bliss of heaven", which showed how near he felt it to be. This is remarkable when we remember that in the Middle Ages it was customary to dwell on the torment to come in order to make men depend upon the Church.

The Authority of the Scriptures

The Bible was, for Wycliffe, the Word of God in every way. He was dedicated to the literal text. He described Christ as the proper author of the Scriptures, and deduced thereby the absolute authority of his work. "As the person of one author is to another, so is the merit of one book to another. Since Christ is infinitely superior to every other man, his book is superior." This being so, he could give no other explanation of the unwillingness of many to acknowledge the authority of Scripture than through their lack of sincere faith in the Lord Jesus Christ himself.

The Sovereignty of God

In the Scriptures he discovered the doctrine of election and embraced it. Bradwardine had taught the Sovereignty of God, but Wycliffe could not agree with him when he appeared to teach that God makes men sin: "if God necessitate man to sin then God is the author of sin", and this could not be. He admired Augustine who also believed in the

Sovereignty of God, but he did not base his predestinarianism upon original sin as Augustine, but on the omnipotence of God. He held to the doctrine of election as firmly as Calvin: "God's goodness is the first cause only why he confers any good on man." Like Calvin, he saw no contradiction between this doctrine and that of human responsibility.

Doctrine of the Church.

Wycliffe came to deny all the distinctive tenets of the Church of Rome. He went further than Luther with regard to the Lord's Supper. What needs to be emphasised above all, however, is the way his thinking developed beyond that of any of the Reformers on the Doctrine of the Church. It was his attitude towards the way in which the Church related to the State that distinguishes him from all the other Reformers. It had a profound practical effect upon him. It could be said of him that he was "the Evangelistic Reformer", because the only alternative to relying on the support of the State, to bring about the changes needed in the Church, was to send out preachers with the Word of God.

Wycliffe had become involved in politics, but only on a temporary basis as an adviser on theological issues. He was ready to recommend to Parliament that they should resist the claims of Rome, and to appeal to Parliament in self- defence; but he believed that the Church should be disendowed (freed from its entanglement with the State). He condemned those he described as the "Caesarean Clergy", who rendered their services to 'Caesar' rather than to Christ, because they were nothing more than civil servants. He wanted the Church to keep clear of "men's law". "Christ's fishers should not meddle with men's law, for men's law containeth sharp stones and trees by which the net of God is broken, and the fish wend out to the world."

He saw the danger of the involvement of ministers in politics, and wanted his preachers to share his view.

> Let men introduced to the care of souls remember how it was with their predecessors in the years before Constantine, with the Master whose name they bear and with the Apostles whom they esteem it their honour to succeed. Let what they solicit from the magistrate be simply protection.

Although this thinking and teaching was revolutionary in England, it *was* Scriptural. He insisted that the voluntary offerings of the people should form the only revenue of the Church. He wanted a return to the state of affairs before Constantine, the Roman Emperor, established Christianity as the official religion of the empire. The enormous wealth of the Church had utterly corrupted it. No-one should be obliged to tithe. Let his preachers depend entirely on the gifts of the people of God.

Wycliffe not only claimed freedom for himself and his 'Bible-Men', but would have given the same freedom to others who disagreed with him. The loss of revenue that would follow his scheme of disendowment would have reduced the clergy to a third of its number but they would have been less corrupt. Henry VIII was glad to use some of Wycliffe's arguments 150 years later when he deprived the Church of its wealth. Wycliffe himself was free from dependence upon the patronage of men of influence. This enabled him to pursue his thinking and writing without restraint. He did not feel obliged to develop a view of church order that would be acceptable to those to whom he was indebted. For him it was simply a question of going back to the Bible.

He had no place for the Doctrine of Development (i.e. that the New Testament allowed for the development of the Church from its simple beginnings). Wycliffe believed that if an institution is not mentioned in the Gospels – for instance, the monastic orders – that is in itself a proof that it is not of divine intent. He anticipated in this the 'regulative principles' of Calvin – that anything that is done in the Church must have Scriptural warrant. It was not enough to say that if a thing was not actually condemned or prohibited it was acceptable.

He gave great liberty to the individual believer. The only check upon his judgment was its conformity to the Scriptures. Baptism and the Lord's Supper could be administered by any true believer. In this he went beyond Luther. He held that in the early church there were only two orders: that Presbyter and Bishop were names of the same office, and that there should be Deacons.

Separation From Rome

In his doctrine of the Church, he considered that the Church consisted only of the regenerate – true believers, "**All who shall be saved in the bliss of heaven are members of the Holy Church and no more.**" He also believed that those who opposed such are "**enemies thereof, and the synagogue of Satan**". In one of his sermons his separatist views come out clearly. He urged his hearers to shun proud men, envious men, back-biters and liars.

> I speak not only of those who are in thy house but wherever thou shalt hear such, shun them and go thou not with such men if thou canst not dissuade them from their error, for by one sickly sheep all the flock is defiled, and a little portion of gall turns much sweetness into bitterness.

To him the church of Rome was utterly false and this led inevitably, in practice, to separation from it.

That church hath been many a day in growing, and some call it not Christ's Church but the church of wicked spirits. A man may no better know Anti-Christ's clerk than by this, that he loveth this church and hateth the Church of Christ [i.e. the true Church].

He urged his followers to have nothing whatever to do with the friars. He personally denounced the Pope as Anti-Christ, and did not spare the prelates because of their false teaching. All this shows us his separatist thinking. The 'gathered church' was clearly not far away, and his followers very soon developed separate congregations, meeting secretly. To him the true church was 'gathered' out of the local community, it was not all those who lived in the parish.

Some have said that he even came to believe in Believers' Baptism, but this does not seem to be the case, though he was accused of denying Infant Baptism. It is true, that he considered that those who believed that infants dying without baptism could not be saved were "presumptuous and foolish". He believed that men were elected by their Maker from the foundation of the world.

It has been asserted by some that he never actually separated from Rome as the other Reformers did. The answer to this charge lies in the fact that he did not believe in setting up an alternative ecclesiastical structure, but simply wanted to be free to preach the Gospel. He simply got on with his tasks and ignored whatever was done to stop him. He anticipated being silenced, as a priest, and his followers were quickly driven underground. He was indeed a separatist in theory and in practice, though when he died he was still, technically, in the Church. It is not without reason that MacFarlane asserted, that his heirs were the 'Brownists', the Elizabethan separatists.

We often see things that are implicit in the teachings of a great man, being logically developed by his disciples. This is certainly true of the Lollards. We can see in them where John Wycliffe's view of the Church was to lead!

10.

The Work that endured.

Chapter One included a surprising quotation from Fox's 'Book of Martyrs'. In it he compared the spiritual condition of the country some four decades after the Reformation had come from Germany with that which existed before we "heard the name of Luther". Fox said things which may be found hard to believe, but the evidence is overwhelming.

According to Fox, the movement which Wycliffe had begun continued, and so prospered that it was only a little inferior in terms of numbers, but much superior in spiritual depth, to the state of affairs after the Reformation had been in progress for some forty years.

New Evidence

Fox was in a position to know the true situation, for he would have had many sources for his material which now no longer survive. However, in recent years ample confirmation of his views has become available. This whole subject is of the greatest importance because it greatly affects our estimate of Wycliffe, and our assessment of the success of his work. When we recognise how much we owe him we shall look with greater interest at his views, his methods, his principles and, above all, his experience of God, as we discover them in his writings.

His Influence on the Continent

His influence on the Continent is reasonably well known. While his books were being burnt in England they were being read in Bohemia. This came about in a wonderful way. When 'Christendom' was divided into two churches, under two popes, the Roman Pope had the support of Bohemia. He was anxious to secure England against the French Pope and so encouraged the marriage between Anne of Bohemia and Richard II. This failed to secure an alliance to suit the Pope, but forged a spiritual link with Bohemia. Queen Anne was a godly woman

Wycliffe's books being burnt at Prague

who loved the Word of God, and through her influence, and contacts between the two royal courts, Wycliffe's works were taken to Bohemia. Wycliffe also influenced Bohemia through Jerome of Prague, who came to Oxford, became devoted to his doctrine, and took back his works to his native land.

In a Bohemian Psalter of 1572 there appears a symbolic picture which shows Wycliffe striking a spark, Huss kindling the coals and Luther brandishing the lighted torch. It has been rightly said that Huss's works were paraphrases of Wycliffe's writings.

It is not surprising that the Council of Constance, which condemned Huss and Jerome to death, should also command Wycliffe's works to be burnt and his grave desecrated.

Wycliffe's influence extended through Huss to Luther, and through Luther back to England. This has been known for many years, but his direct influence through his followers upon the English Reformation has been greatly underestimated. Even more significant is his influence upon English Puritanism and seventeenth century Nonconformity.

The Lollards

After Wycliffe's death, nearly thirty years passed before the authorities persecuted the Lollards with any real severity. There were many in high places that had genuine sympathy with Wycliffe's views, but few who would face the inevitable storm. In 1395, a bold attempt was made by Privy Counsellors to influence Parliament along the lines of Wycliffe's views, but the King forced them to back down. The numbers of sympathisers and adherents to the Lollard cause was such, however, that their enemies could not strike them down with one blow. It was not until Henry IV came to the throne in 1412 that persecution of the worst kind began.

The law for the burning of heretics had been passed in 1401. This condemned their "wicked preaching, new doctrines, unlawful conventicles" and their schools and books, "in which they wickedly instruct and inform the people". In the past it had not been rigourously enforced, but it now began to be with the accession of the new king. This had its effect upon those of the gentry who followed Wycliffe. His colleagues at Oxford had given way, and the higher-class Lollards were soon to yield. There were some noble exceptions. The testimony of Sir John Oldcastle, Lord Cobham, was noteworthy, and he was prepared to go to the flames.

We may be tempted to compare the martyrs of the fifteenth century with those of the sixteenth who were more prepared to face the flames. Many in the fifteenth century did recant, but the whole concept of martyrdom was altogether new. Englishmen had never contemplated an alternative religion. Not one

Lord Cobham preaching

in ten thousand had any idea of what the French Dissenters (the Albigensians), or the Italians (the Waldensians), had believed and suffered. The idea of dissent was totally new.

Their Strength

Persecution gradually reduced the number of Wycliffe's followers amongst the upper classes, leaving mostly those from the lower ranks of society. It is for this reason that their strength has been underestimated. They met secretly, but did have a loose association among themselves. They had Wycliffe's Bible, and some of his works, but above all they loved the Gospel itself.

Trevelyan, when describing an opponent of the Lollards, gives us an idea of the strength of the movement:

His language implies that he was not speaking merely of a small sect, despised and rejected of men, but an attitude of mind which a clergyman might expect to find prevailing to greater or lesser degree wherever he went. Even in the darkest days Lollardy was leavening society and causing great uneasiness to its enemies.

Their Doctrines Similar to Wycliffe's

Like Wycliffe they held that nothing is to be regarded as the law of God unless founded on Scripture, and that every Christian can expect to arrive at a proper understanding of Scripture. When this has been discovered all human arguments are to be rejected. Wycliffe's puritanism had made him complain about religious entertainment:

God forbid that any Christian man understand that this censing and crying that men use now be the best service of a priest and most profitable to a man's soul. It seems that we seek much in liking and pride in this song more than the devotion and understanding of that which we sing, and this is great sin.

Similar words were written by one of his followers in 1400, "priests in the churches give themselves so much to song and so little to preaching".

We are told that,

In the devotion of the Lollards to the vernacular Scriptures the link with Wycliffe is very strong, they were still saying and practising at the beginning of the sixteenth century what he had been saying and practising at the end of the fourteenth – that all good doctrine must be grounded in the Bible. They carried on his emphasis on Scripture right to the Reformation.

The Lollards, like Wycliffe, opposed the elaborate ornamentation of buildings, and extravagant music and, according to Stacey,

Lord Cobham being burnt

believed in "rigid sabbatarianism".

When we read the examinations of the Lollards we see just how much they were like the later puritans both in doctrine and practice.

Walter Brute, one of the early Lollards, when tried, sent a manuscript to court in answer to the bishop's summons: "Rome is the daughter of Babylon, the great whore sitting upon many waters, with whom the kings of the earth have committed fornication, with her enchantments, witchcraft and Simon Magus' merchandise, the whole world is infected and seduced." He prophesied her fall in the language of Revelation. The Pope is "the Beast ascending out of the earth, having two horns like a lamb", who compels "small and great, rich and poor, to worship the Beast, to take his mark on their forehead and on their hands".

As we might expect, the Lollard preachers also attacked transubstantiation, image worship, prayers for the dead, and confessions, because these gave great power to the clergy. They also denounced exorcism, and blessings continually performed on inanimate objects, as being necromancy. Like Wycliffe they saw the Pope as Anti-Christ and regarded him as the "common scandal of the world". They believed that men should live like the Apostles, content with simple food and dress.

Their Conduct

When we consider not only what they believed, but how they lived, we might well think we were reading about the non-conformists of the seventeenth century with their stress, like Wycliffe, on devotional and personal morality. They were described as:

men of a serious, modest deportment; they avoid all ostentation in dress, mix little with the busy world, and complain of the debauchery of mankind. They maintain themselves entirely by their own labour, despising wealth, being fully content with mere necessaries. They follow no trade, because it is attended with so much lying, swearing and cheating. They are chaste and temperate, never seen in taverns, nor amused by vain pleasures.

You find them always employed, either learning or teaching. They are concise and devout in their prayers, blaming lifeless tediousness [i.e. vain repetition in prayer]. They never swear, they speak little; in public preaching they lay the chief stress upon charity [love]. They disregard the canonical hours, saying that the Lord's prayer repeated with devotion is better than tedious hours (Romish services) without devotion. They explain the Scriptures differently from the interpretations of the holy doctors and church of Rome. They speak little, and with humility; they are well behaved in appearance.

Their Influence on the Reformation

Burrows remarks upon the effect of Wycliffe's followers on the Reformation. He recognised the factors that are usually referred to, such as the Renaissance, Henry VIII's divorce and Luther, but draws attention to:

the gradual education of the English people, which had been steadily proceeding beneath the surface of society ever since Wiclif's time. It is not too much to say that it saved the English Reformation from the extravagances and errors which naturally sprang from the comparative suddenness of the change elsewhere.

We are all, in short, familiar enough with the fact that it was through the powerful impulse given by Wiclif's works that the principles of the Reformation made their way in Bohemia, from thence (through the foul proceedings of the Council of Constance) to all Europe, and becoming transplanted into the German mind, that they assisted Luther in bringing about the Reformation with which we associate his name. But the circumstances we have reviewed have contributed to obscure the equally certain fact of the irrepressible growth and steady development of these principles for generations, through Wiclif's works, in England itself; and the history of the English Reformation is unintelligible without it.

Gradual Increase

The Lollard movement did not slowly decline as the years passed, but rather increased. It was not as though a besieged and beleaguered garrison held out until reinforcements came from another part; on the contrary, an army was steadily growing and winning! The work of God was growing with a quickening pace shortly before the Reformation came to our shores from Germany. The forces of the Reformation in England were reaching bounds that have only been appreciated in recent years . Modern research has vindicated Fox, and also Trevelyan (who wrote at the beginning of our century). The nineteenth century saw great interest in Wycliffe because his writings, previously unpublished, became available. Scholars began to give him his proper place. Trevelyan puts it like this:

The ideas of Latimer and Luther did not come to Englishmen in all the shocking violence of novelty [completely new teaching] since here the doctrines of Lollardy had been common talk ever since 1380. The doctrinal and ritual reformation of religion in England was not a work of the sixteenth century alone. The Englishman moves slowly, cautiously and often silently. The movement began with Wycliffe. England was not converted from Germany; she changed her own opinion and had begun that process long before Wittenburg or Geneva became famous in theological controversy. If we take a general view of our religious history we must hold that English Protestantism had a gradual and lengthy regular growth.

The English people reading Wycliffe's Bible – George Clausen R.A.
(from the painting in St Stephen's Hall, Westminster, reproduced by kind permission of Mr. Speaker)

We must now consider the historical evidence which is at the basis of such statements.

Lollard Trials

It was hard for these early Non-conformists. They were condemned not only for denying transubstantiation and other Roman doctrines, but for other matters, too. It was a criminal offence to copy the Bible, to read it, or even hear it read! The magnificent painting by Clausen, 'The English People Reading the Wycliffe Bible' (which hangs in St. Stephen's Hall, Palace of Westminster), is expertly done. It shows a group of people, from all classes, reading out of doors, but in secret. One of their number is keeping watch. Clausen was commissioned to paint a series on the long struggle of the English people for the religious liberty accomplished after many years of heroic endurance.

We learn about both the size of the 'underground' Lollard movement and its beliefs, from the records of these trials. We can easily and quickly see its very large proportions, and its doctrines.

The Size of the Movement

In 1431, the Bishop of Bath and Wells threatened with excommunication anyone throughout Somerset who translated or copied the Bible. He was evidently having serious troubles. In the East too, there was trouble for the bishops. Near Beccles, on the border of Norfolk and Suffolk, great congregations were discovered, and Lollard schools as well. Arrangements had also been made to smuggle the latest heretical tracts from London. This was done by middle-class individuals. The Bishop of Norwich attempted to break up these congregations, and tried over 100 people. Some were condemned for simply reading the Bible.

A Lollard preacher named Thomas Mann, before being burned in 1518, told his judges that he believed he had converted 700 persons in the course of his life. Mann had found at Newbury "a glorious and sweet society of faithful followers who had continued the space of 15 years till betrayed". He also found at Amersham "a godly and a great company which had continued in that doctrine and teaching 23 years". In 1521 a "secret multitude of true professors" was discovered in the Chiltern Hills. Over 300 people were accused in Buckingham. In the same year the Bishop of London arrested 500 Lollards. At Ashford in Kent, 46 'heretics' were condemned in 1511.

Congregations were growing all over the country. Uxbridge and Henley had congregations in close contact with the East Anglians not long before Luther appeared on the scene. In 1521 a great attack was made on them, together with those in Essex and Middlesex. Hundreds of people were condemned. They had in their possession

Lollard Tower (prison)

Wycliffe's Bible and his 'Wicket' (which condemns transubstantiation). There are no references whatever to Continental influences. The Bishop of Lincoln had over 200 'heretics' brought before him. Wycliffe's followers were all over the country.

Persecutions in the early sixteenth century reveal connections between the London Protestants and their predecessors of the previous century. When Lutheranism did arrive in England in 1523 Tunstall, the Bishop of London, wrote to Erasmus: "It is no question of some pernicious novelty. It is only that new arms are being added to the great band of Wycliffite heretics."

Dickens wrote about the Lollards in the diocese of York in the early sixteenth century. He asserts that the Reformation "did not originate as a mere foreign doctrine, imported by a handful of intellectuals and mysteriously imposed by the monarchy against the almost unanimous wishes of a Catholic nation. The foreign seed fell upon a ground prepared for its reception, and prepared by something more than anticlericalism or royal propaganda." Records "resemble the visible portions of an iceberg".

Growth Right up to the Reformation

The movement was far from dying out before the Reformation came from Germany. It was increasing, and this increase was independent of Continental influence.

Anabaptists from Europe were few and far between, and did not survive long in England. An ever-increasing number of men were being burnt for Lollardy. It even led to a complaint by Henry VIII's secretary in 1511, in a letter to Erasmus, that wood had grown scarce and dear because so much was needed to burn heretics, "and yet their numbers grow". Those who suffered, too, in Mary's reign, were from areas where Lollards were the strongest.

Scotland

It is not surprising that Lollards should have been found in Scotland as well as England. They were not in such large numbers, but continued right until the Reformation, as in England. Complaint was made in 1415 that heretics "who claim that their sayings are founded on Holy Scripture and on its literal sense, and who say that they follow and recognise Scripture only, are present in England, have destroyed the University of Prague, and have reached over Scotland". Burnings for Lollardy were recorded in 1422 and 1432, and in 1494 thirty Lollards were discovered in Kyle, whose views differed little from those of Wycliffe.

In 1520 Purvey's revision of Wycliffe's New Testament was "read in the kirk upon certain days of the year", put into the Scots dialect by Murdoch Nisbet. He had become a Lollard in about 1500 and fled overseas in 1513. He made a copy of the New Testament and returned home. Because of his danger "he built a vault at the bottom of his own house, to which he retired himself, serving God and reading his new book". Two of his companions were burnt at Glasgow in 1539, and one of his descendants, John Nisbet of Hardhill, was executed as a Covenanter in 1685. Patrick Hamilton was not the first in Scotland to profess the Protestant faith. John Knox called Kyle "an old receptacle to the servants of God".

Lollardy was not as influential in Scotland as in England, but there can be no doubt that it had a valuable part to play in the Scottish Reformation.

The Doctrine of the Lollards

The strength of this now confident movement may surprise us, but their beliefs may surprise us still more. Congregations met in secret and read Wycliffe's Bible and those few of his works that had escaped the flames. In 1400 a book was written which is of particular interest as it throws light on the way Wycliffe's followers thought of the Church. Called 'The Lantern of Light', it divided 'the Church' into three parts. The first, the true Church, is that part that "only belongs to God; that was chosen in the time of grace by the water of cleansing, by Christ's blood of redemption and by the power of the Holy Ghost". The second is the "material Church" (i.e. the building made for worship); the third is the "priests' Church". Directions are given to "know the good from the evil", i.e. to recognise this third church; and a detailed description of how opposite the members of the first and third are to each other (i.e. the regenerate and unregenerate) is given. The non-conformist church was developing quickly.

William Thorpe, in his trial before Archbishop Arundel in 1407, declared his concept of the church, which clearly foreshadowed the whole concept of the 'gathered church'. It was not the church established by law; its boundaries were not the same as the whole community, but 'gathered out' from the local population.

> Therefore I believe that the gathering together of this people, living now here in this life, is the holy church of God, fighting here on earth against the fiend, the ·prosperity of the world and their fleshly lusts. Wherefore, seeing that all the gathering together of this church . . . loveth not but to do his pleasing . . . I submit myself unto this holy church of Christ.

Clearly, Non-conformity had begun in the fifteenth century.

One of the delightful titles given to the Lollards was the 'Known Ones'. This refers to the care they had in acquainting themselves with one another before receiving them into the brotherhood.

The Lollards' Puritan views have already been referred to, but Dickens sees a connection between actual congregations: "The communities which displayed the most marked Lollard tendency before 1558 proceeded in each case to develop Puritan tendencies in Elizabethan and Jacobean times." He goes on to connect Lollardy with seventeenth century Independency.

Baptists

In Tewkesbury, the Baptist Church actually traces its origin to the Lollard period. There is a notice of this in the old church building which says,

> The influence of Wycliffe was very strong in this part of the country. There was a strong Lollard community in the district around. Many of the Lollards observed the rite of Believers' Baptism. Some local authorities are of the opinion that the Tewkesbury Baptist Church is really a continuation of Lollard community. In 1540 Thomas Ransford was born in the locality, and he became a Baptist. A 1623 deed conveying property is in existence, and a 1655 Minute Book and records of a well-established chapel with 120 members are held in a safe in the present day Baptist Church.

Amersham memorial

Large, strong Baptist congregations emerged in areas where the Lollards had been strongest, especially in South Buckinghamshire. A Bristol weaver, James Willis, was a fervent missionary, and had put new heart into congregations at Wycombe, Amersham and Chesham, besides winning new converts at Henley, Marlow, Hambledon, Turville and Chinnor. It is evident that he was a Baptist as one of his flock at Henley believed that no man ought to be baptised until he was mature. An unbroken tradition connects the Henley congregation with the seventeenth century Non-conformists of the Chiltern Hills.

Other examples of Baptist views can be cited. In 1457, a Baptist congregation was discovered in Chesterton (according to the Bishop of Ely). The sudden growth of Baptists in the days of Mary and Elizabeth is further proof of the doctrine held by Lollard congregations.

Continental Anabaptists had little influence in England because of the unorthodox views of many of them. "Bishop Jewel intimates at the beginning of Queen Elizabeth's reign that there were few of them." At the same time, "the Puritans, it is certain, held their principles of separation both at the beginning of her reign and afterward". (Lewis). These separatist congregations had developed from Lollard meetings and would become, in many cases, Baptist churches in the following century.

Blending with the Reformation

On the Continent there was a continual tension between the Anabaptists and the Reformed Churches, whereas in England it was different. Lollards took a great interest in the new teaching from Europe. At Oxford, John Colet had received Protestant doctrine from Europe and was teaching it from the pulpit of the established church. The Lollards eagerly listened to him, "nodding and exchanging glances during his sermon". Thomas Bilney, like Colet, was similarly enlightened and he was also given a warm reception in East Anglia. This is not surprising since John Wycliffe's whole view of salvation was identical with that of the other Reformers. He believed it was a sovereign work of God. The Continental Anabaptists did not believe this. They gave a place to human co-operation in salvation. In this they differed fundamentally from the Reformers. The way in which the old and the new blended and the enormous debt the new owed to the old has recently been documented.

Recent Research

In 1983 a monograph by John F. Davis was published by the Royal Historical Society on 'Heresy and Reformation in the South East of England, 1520-1559'. This recent work gives striking support to all that has been said by earlier historians, and adds important new evidence. Dr. Davis rejects the accounts of the Reformation in England that place the emphasis on the theological influence of the continental reformers and the political ends of the English Government, and ignore the strength of Lollardy. He discovered, in his research, "a powerful native strand in the events, deriving in part from Lollardy, which provided the reformed religion with a prepared breeding ground, and strongly influenced all subsequent developments".

His evidence is most instructive: "Lollardy was a gathered church, and discovered in definite localities, preserving well-marked traditions of belief." It was in these very areas that Protestantism first flourished. Lollard antecedents underlay centres of Puritanism and actual underground gatherings became Puritan congregations. This happened when "Puritan leaders in London" held pastoral charge "in the part of the metropolis where the old Lollard conventicles had flourished, in particular St. Giles, Cripplegate, and All Hallows, Honey Lane".

Lollard congregations in Norfolk that flourished in the fifteenth century were still strong in the early sixteenth century, when hundreds of them were arrested. There are many connections between continuing fifteenth century Lollard meetings and sixteenth century trials of those who were being considered 'Protestant'.

What is particularly interesting is the way in which the followers of Wycliffe not only provided support for those within the established Church who were receiving the New Light from the Continent, but actually had an effect on their thinking.

Much has been attributed to the influence of Luther which properly belongs to Wycliffe. A careful examination of the views of Tyndale show that, in some respects, he owed more to the Lollards than to Luther. "The reception of Lutheranism in England took place more in the imagination of the bishops than in reality." The charges against those suspected of Lutheranism show that they were condemned for mainly Lollard views. Thomas Bilney, though initially influenced by continental ideas, was himself affected by Wycliffe's disciples. "The old Lollard beliefs coloured Bilney's Evangelism [Evangelicalism]." According to Davis "he stands in line with Wycliffe".

There were close contacts between those who were within the Church and coming to a Protestant position and the older movement. Miles Coverdale encouraged a converted friar to join a local Lollard meeting. These Protestants within the Church were less influenced by Luther and more by Wycliffe's followers than has been assumed. They had "some acquaintance with Luther's doctrines but the effect of these was secondary and at best commonly superficial".

Fox was anxious to confirm the link between the Reformers and the earlier (Lollard) Protestants, to show the continuity of the Reformed movement. He not only chronicled their suffering but, together with Bale, republished many of their writings. The two movements were not so far apart that they could not come together but, inevitably, there was a desire among the Lollards for a more radical and Biblical Reformation than the English Monarchy would allow. The Lollards were puritan at heart and would not be satisfied with the 'Elizabethan Settlement' (or rather, compromise).

Puritan Non-conformity

Thomson, in his 'Later Lollards', says that "by the time the Roman establishment was succeeded by the Anglican, Lollardy was developing into Puritanism". English Puritanism had a character of its own, and when it failed to change the Church of England it developed during the seventeenth century into Non-conformity. According to the greatest authority on Wycliffe, Workman, "the Anglican Settlement owed little directly to Wycliffe's influence. He should be regarded as the fore-runner and the father of the Puritans, Covenanters and Non-conformists of Great Britain and America."

The emergence of large numbers of congregations that were independent, self-governing and, in many cases, Baptist, yet at the same time thoroughly Reformed in their view of salvation, was unique to English soil. The reason for this must surely be found in the faith of John Wycliffe. His Doctrine of Salvation, that gave no place to human merit at any point, and his concept of the church as a truly voluntary community of the people of God, had its ultimate fulfilment in great numbers of congregations that were both non-conformist in their view of the church and puritan in their theology. These have spread to North America and to every part of the globe. His ashes, emblem of his doctrine, have truly reached the four corners of the world.

11.

Wycliffe's Word to us.

The object of this book is not just to furnish an interesting insight into our history, or to blame, as Milton did, those who silenced Wycliffe, but to learn lessons that will help us in our present situation – because "there is nothing new under the sun".

Milton's verdict on Wycliffe is striking:

> Had it not been the obstinate perverseness of our prelates against the divine and admirable spirit of Wycliffe to suppress him as a schismatic and innovator, perhaps neither the Bohemian Huss and Jerome – no, nor the names of Luther or of Calvin – had ever been known. The glory of reforming all our neighbours had been completely ours.

Milton's patriotism is evident. We can look back and see lessons that can be learned because spiritual battles were fought and won that have to be repeated all over again.

We do not have to ask ourselves the question, "What would Wycliffe say to us today?", because he has written so much that is so applicable. We can let him speak for himself. Spiritually, there are real parallels with the pre-Reformation scene. Our heritage has been sold by those who, like Esau, do not value their inheritance. The Word of God has been losing its place in the life of the churches, and is being replaced by religious entertainment. Men still preach, but their preaching has been getting more and more like that of those who Wycliffe was constantly opposing; and now even the preaching itself is giving way to other forms of communication. The friar-preachers had to compete with the religious dramatist, and eventually, with the elaborate singing.

Evangelism

Wycliffe knew that only the Word of God could change men's hearts. It was the *'Divine Seed'*! He applied the dictum Sola Scriptura comprehensively. He not only rejected all human tradition in doctrine and practice in the life of the church, but in evangelism too. How easy it would have been for him to say that the people were not capable of receiving a spoken or written message. They were ignorant, uneducated, and used to being entertained; but Wycliffe gave them only the Word of God. He was careful, however, to accommodate himself to his hearers' capacity. He did not advocate long and heavy sermons. He could have indulged his academic talent, but instead sought the edification of his hearers.

Experience

Wycliffe was not only a brilliant man, but his personal knowledge of God was outstanding. His sermon, 'The Love of Jesus', indicates that he had a sense of the love of God that few have ever experienced. This helps us to understand how he could continue, to his last breath, a life of consistent and faithful witnessing. He was sustained in his personal life and in his warfare against the enemies of the Gospel, even when he was a physical wreck and facing martyrdom.

The Lollard movement has a parallel in our day in Soviet Russia, where underground churches are continually harassed, yet are growing. They are denied attractive and expensive methods of evangelism. Their weapon is the Word of God. Their advertisements are their lives. It was so 600 years ago in England.

The Scriptures

John Wycliffe was used by Almighty God to move England out of the Dark Ages almost to the Reformation itself. He did it with the Word of God *alone*. His remarkable discovery of so much truth amidst so much darkness can be understood in the light of the Scripture: "If any man will do his will he shall understand the doctrine." (John 7:17) He was ready to obey the light he was given, and so he received more. He understood, too, that "the object of the commandment is love out of a pure heart and faith unfeigned", (1 Tim.1:5). He did not want to use the Scriptures to establish a reputation for himself, but to edify his hearers. No one could have done this more than he, with all his scholastic skill, but he set it aside for the benefit of those who needed the simple Gospel. It had had its effect on him, and he saw that it was designed to have its effect on others. He applied it to his own life, and insisted on personal godliness. He taught it, translated it, and sent out his 'Bible-Men'.

The book of James was a favourite with his

followers, but this does not mean they did not preach a gospel of faith. Wycliffe may not have urged men to be saved in the same way as Whitefield or Spurgeon, but the truth was all there and had its effect. In a message on 'The Charter of our Heavenly Heritage' there is a clear sense of urgency in his words. Salvation is not a process – men must seek the Lord, and the moment they turn fully, God saves them. "Whatever day or hour a sinful man or woman leave their sin, wholly, and heartily, with bitter sorrow, and turn to him, he shall receive them in his mercy."

Sola Scriptura

The spiritual situation was desperate 600 years ago, a fact that was apparent to those who had spiritual understanding. This may not have been the view of those who were doing very well out of the spiritual chaos. The friars were well rewarded for "stuffing the people with garbage", and the religious entertainers would have been well pleased with the great numbers that heard and watched their performances. Those who judged the situation by the rule of God's Word actually thought that the devil was "let loose" (according to Revelation 20), but this belief did not paralyse them. It made them look to God alone, and obey his Word. They spoke his Word with an astonishing and costly boldness. The promises of his Word have been fulfilled, and we have been the beneficiaries.

If it is proper, helpful and Scriptural to make parallels with former ages, there is much to learn from Master John Wycliffe. His confidence in the Word of God, and the Word alone, was vindicated by the One who gave it and put it into his heart. Let us have a similar confidence.

12.

Wycliffe's Sermons.

Some may find this last chapter the most profitable and impressive because they can hear Wycliffe speaking to them personally. He is known almost entirely by his own writings, so many of which have been preserved, yet very little of a personal nature was recorded. It has been said that he is known by his works because "no other record has been left of him except by the abuse from his enemies". However, we can learn a great deal from what he wrote.

It is of especial interest to see how often he refers to faith, and in particular, the "bliss of heaven". His experience of "the love of Jesus" is quite evident from his own writings, and helps us to understand how he could battle on to the very end, though few men with influence in the country would stand with him. Some of the messages which are included here are taken from 'The Poor Caitiff'

(wretched man). It is a volume of small tracts, written in English and widely circulated, although each copy had to be hand-written.

Wycliffe's sermons are frequently only sketches or outlines of his actual discourses. More than 300 have been preserved and were, most likely, taken down by some of his hearers at Lutterworth. This could well have been done by John Purvey, his curate. It is evident that they were given as examples for others to follow, which they did.

All the messages have been abbreviated in varying degrees, but *not paraphrased*. The spelling, of course, has been modernised, and some archaic wording updated, but the words are substantially the very ones used by Wycliffe. We begin with advice given by him to his followers:

The gospel telleth us the duty which falls to all the disciples of Christ, and

also telleth us how priests, both high
and low, should occupy themselves in
the church of God and in serving him.
And first, Jesus himself did do the
lessons which he taught. The gospel
relates how Jesus went about in the
places of the country, both great and
small, as in cities and castles, or small
towns; and this is to teach us to be
useful generally to men, and not to be
unwilling to preach to a people
because they are few, and our name
may not, in consequence, be great. For
we should labour for God, and from
him hope for our reward. There is no
doubt that Christ went into small
uplandish towns, as to Bethphage, and
Cana in Galilee; for Christ went to all
those places where he wished to do
good. And he laboured not thus for
gain, for he was not smitten either with
pride or with covetousness.

**The pulpit at Lutterworth part of which is considered
contemporary with Wycliffe**

A Selection of Wycliffe's Sermons

Sermon One: 'On The Belief'

The ground of all goodness is stedfast faith, or belief. This, through grace and mercy, is obtained from God. Faith was the principal ground that enabled the woman of Canaan to obtain health of soul and of body from Christ, for her daughter, who was evil treated by a devil, as the gospel relates. And the centurion was much praised of Christ for the stedfast belief that he had in the power of his Godhead. Faith is likened to the north star, for it showeth the haven of grace to men rowing in the sea of this world. Faith is the eastern star that leads spiritual kings to worship Jesus Christ.

Faith or belief is as a stone lying in the foundation of a strong building, that beareth up all the work. For as the building standeth firmly that is well grounded upon a stone, so each virtuous deed is strong when it is grounded upon the solidity of belief. For upon this stone, that is, solid faith, Christ said that he would build his church, that is, man's soul.

A man that hath lost his right eye is unable to defend himself in battle, for his shield hides his left eye, and so he has no sight to defend himself from his enemy; even so he that has lost the right eye of true faith, is unable to withstand or fight against his spiritual enemy, the devil. Saints, as St Paul saith, through stedfastness and true faith overcame kingdoms, Heb. 11.

The lack of stedfast faith is the chief reason why men fall into deadly sin. Christ said to his disciples, that if their faith were as great as the seed of mustard, and they should say to this hill: "Move from here", it should move; and nothing should be impossible to them.

While Peter had true faith, he walked upon the sea as upon dry land; but when the firmness of his faith failed, he began to sink, and therefore Christ reproved him for being of little faith. So it is with us, who are staggering and unstedfast with the wind of each temptation or fear.

Therefore, brethren, let us set all our belief and full trust on him who is almighty, and not in any vain thing that may fail in any time. We must trust stedfastly that nothing may harm us any more than he will allow it, and all things which he sendeth come for the best. And let no wealth of this failing world, neither tribulation, draw our hearts from firm belief in God. Let us not put our belief or trust in charms, or in dreams, or any other fantasies; but only in Almighty God.

To believe in God, as St Augustine saith, is: in belief to cleave to God through love, and to seek busily to fulfil his will; for no man truly believeth in God, except he that loveth God. And no man sinneth against God except when he fails in belief, which is the ground of all good works.

Knight ready for battle

Sermon Two:
'The Armour Of Heaven'

St Paul saith, "Clothe yourselves in the armour of God, that ye may firmly stand against temptations and deceits of the Fiend." Man's body is like clothes with which his soul is covered; and as a horse that bears his master through many perils. And from this horse, that is man's body, many things, are required, if he will bear his master aright out of perils.

For no knight can safely fight against his enemy, unless his horse be obedient to him; no more can the soul fight against the wiles of the Fiend, if the flesh, which is his horse, live in lusts and likings at his own will.

For Holy Scripture saith, "He that nourisheth his servant", that is, his own body, "delicately or lustfully, shall find it rebel when he least expecteth." As soon as man begins to live wisely, and flees all the lusts and desires, and vanities, which he before was used to and loved, and bows himself under the yoke of God's holy doctrine, then his enemies begin to contrive by wiles, frauds, and temptations, to make him fall. And therefore it is needful that his horse be submissive and helping his master to overcome his enemies. For if the soul and the body be well agreed together, and either of them helps the other in this spiritual contest, the Fiend shall soon flee and be overcome. For Holy Scripture saith, "Withstand ye the Fiend, and he shall flee from you."

But it were great folly for any man to fight upon an unbridled horse, and if the horse be wild and ill taught, the bridle must be heavy, and the bit sharp, to hold him again. And if the horse be easy and obedient to his master, his bridle shall be light and smooth also.

This bridle is called abstinence, with which the body shall be restrained, that he have not all his own way, for he is wild and wilful, and loth to bow to goodness. With this bridle, his master shall restrain him, to be meek and bow to his will. For if he will fight without a bridle upon him, it is impossible for him not to fall.

But this bridle of abstinence should be led by wisdom, so that nature be held by strength, and the wildness of our nature be restrained by this bridle. For otherwise his horse will fail at the greatest need, and harm his master, and make him lose his victory.

This bridle must have two strong reins, by which thou mayest direct thy horse at thy will; also they must be even, and neither pass the other in length. For if thou drawest one faster than the other, thy horse will swerve aside, and go out of the way. Therefore, if thy horse shall stay in the middle of the way, it is necessary to draw the reins of thy bridle even.

The one rein of thy bridle is too loose, when thou allowest thy flesh to have its will too much, in eating and drinking, in speaking, in sleeping, in idle standing or sitting, and trivial tale telling, and all other things that the flesh desires beyond measure and reason. The other rein of the bridle is held too tight when thou art too stern with thine own body and withdrawest from it that which it should reasonably have.

Whoso pulleth either of these reins uneven, will make his horse swerve aside and lose the right way. If thou allowest thy body to have its full liking, that which should be thy friend becomes thy decided foe. If thou withholdest therefrom that which it ought to have to sustain its nature, as its need requires, then thou destroyest its strength and its might, so that it cannot help thee as it should. Therefore sustain thy horse, that it faint not, nor fail at thy need. And withdraw from it that which might turn thee to folly.

Yet thy horse needs to have a saddle, to sit upon him the more securely and gracefully in other men's sight. This saddle is gentleness or easiness. That is, whatsoever thou doest, be it done with good consideration; wisely thinking it through from the beginning to the ending, and what may happen as result; and that it be done sweetly and meekly, and with gentleness. That is, that thou calmly suffer slanders and scorns, and other harms that men do against thee, and neither grieve thyself in word nor in deed. And though thy flesh be aggrieved, keep calmness in heart, and let not any wicked words come from thy mouth or tongue, and then thou shalt be made glad.

As the prophet saith, "The calm and the submissively suffering shall result in joy for ever for those who do gently with easiness and love, whatsoever they do; so that their outward and inward semblance and cheer, be so gentle and lovely in word and deed, that others may be turned to good by their example." This virtue, gentleness of heart and of appearance, makes man gracious to God, and attractive to man's sight, as a saddle makes a horse attractive and praiseable.

Two spurs it is needful that thou have for thy horse, and that they be sharp to prick thy horse if needful, that he loiter not in his way; for many horses are slow if they be not spurred. These two spurs are love and dread;

which of all things most stir men to the way of heaven.

The right spur is the love that God's dear children have for the lasting prosperity that shall never end. The left spur is dread of the pains of hell, which are without number, and never may be counted out. With these two spurs prick thy horse if he be dull and unwilling to stir himself to good. And if the right spur of love be not sharp enough to make him go forward on his journey, prick him with the left spur of dread to rouse him.

Separate thy soul from thy body by inward thought, and send thy heart before, into that other land [heaven]; and do as a man would do that must choose between two dwelling places into which when he had once entered he must dwell for ever. Certainly, if he were wise, he would send before some of his near friends to see what these places were.

Two places are ordained for man to dwell in after this life. While he is here, he may choose, by God's mercy, which he will; but once he has gone from here he may not do so. For whichever he first goes to, whether he like it well or ill, there he must dwell for evermore. He shall never after change his dwelling, though he hates it ever so badly. Heaven and hell are these two places, and in one of them, each man must dwell.

In heaven is more joy than may be told with tongue, or thought with heart; and in hell is more pain than any man may suffer. With these two spurs awake thou thy horse, and send thy heart before, as a secret friend, to espy these dwelling places, what they are.

In hell thou shalt find all that heart may hate, empty of all good, plenty of all evil that may hurt any thing in body or in soul. – Hot fire burning, darkness, brimstone most offensive, foul storms and tempests, greedy devils, open mouthed as raging lions, hunger and thirst that never shall be quenched – there is weeping, and wailing, and gnashing of teeth, and thick darkness. All hate each other as the foul Fiend, and constantly curse the time that they wrought sin.

Above all things they desire to die, and they are ever dying, and fully die they never shall, but ever dying live in pain and woe. They hated death while they lived here, but now they would rather have it than all the wide world. They shall think upon no good, and have no knowledge but of their pains, and sins that they have done. And of all these pains, and many more sorrows than we can tell, end shall never come.

When thou understandest that the deadly sin which man has done, shall be paid for so dearly with that everlasting pain: then thou wouldest desire rather to let thy skin be torn from thy flesh, and thy body hewn to pieces, than that thou wouldest wilfully do a deadly sin – this spur of dread shall make our horse awake, and keep him in the right way, and speed him fast forward, and cause him always to flee from deadly sin, which is thus dearly bought, and maketh man to be thus bitterly pained for ever.

And this is the right spur that should quicken thy horse to speed in his way; that thou learn to love Jesus Christ, in all thy living. And therefore send thou thy thoughts into that land of life, where no disease is, of any kind; neither age nor sickness, nor any other grievance. And whoso goeth there shall find a gracious fellowship; the orders of angels, and of all holy saints, and the Lord above them, who gladdeneth them all.

There is plenty of all good, and absence of all things that may grieve. There are fairness and riches, honour and joy that each man may feel; love and wisdom that shall last for ever. There is no disease that men suffer here; not hypocrisy nor flattery, nor falsehood, envy and ire. Banished from there are thieves and tyrants, cruel and greedy men that pillage the poor, proud men and boasters, covetous and beguilers, slothful and licentious, all such are banished out of that pure land.

For there is nothing that men may fear, but instead pleasure and joy and mirth at will, melody and song of angels, bright and lasting bliss that never shall cease. And though they were sick and feeble while they lived here, they shall be so strong there, that nothing shall move against their will. They shall have such great freedom that nothing shall be contrary to their liking. The saved bodies shall never have sickness, nor anger nor grievance.

Also they shall be filled with joy in all their senses; for as a vessel that is dipped in water or other liquid, is wet within and without, above and beneath, and also all about, and no more liquid can be within it, even so shall those that are saved, be full filled with all joy and bliss. Also they shall have endless life in the sight of the Holy Trinity, and this joy shall pass all other. They shall be in full security, that they will never lose that joy, nor be put out thereof. They shall see him, both God and man, and they shall see themselves in him also. They shall also have perfect love to each other, for every one shall agree with the other's desire. And these joys and many more than any tongue of man can fully tell, shall those have that shall be saved, both in body and soul, after the day of doom. [judgement]

This is the right spur, which should stir men joyfully to love Jesus Christ, and to hasten in the heavenly way. For so sweet is the bliss there, and so great withal, that whoever tastes a single drop of it, would be so rapt in liking of God, and of heavenly joy, and he would have such a longing to go there, that all the joy of the world would seem pain to him. This love would move such a man to live more virtuously, and to flee from sin, a hundred times more than any dread of the pain of hell. For perfect love putteth out all dread, and cleanseth the soul from filth, and maketh it to see God, and to flee oft to heaven in its desires, hoping to dwell there, for ever.

Sermon Three: 'To Love Jesus'

Whosoever thou art that desireth to love God, if thou wilt neither be deceived nor deceive, if thou wilt be saved and not fail, if thou wilt stand and not fall, study to have this name *Jesus* constantly in mind. If thou doest so the enemy shall fall, and thou shalt stand, the enemy shall be enfeebled, and thou shalt be strengthened – therefore seek this name, *Jesus*, hold it and forget it not. Nothing so quenches flames, restrains evil thoughts, cuts away venomous affections, or alienates from us vain occupations.

This name, *Jesus*, truly held in mind, rooteth up vices, planteth virtues, bringeth charity or love to men, giveth men a taste of heavenly things, removeth discord, produceth peace, giveth everlasting rest, and doeth away with fleshly desires. All earthly desires, all earthly things, it turneth into heaviness. It filleth those that love it with spiritual joy. The righteous deserveth to be blessed, for he hath truly loved this name, *Jesus*. He is called righteous, because he seeks earnestly to love *Jesus*. What can go wrong for him who unceasingly yearns to love *Jesus*? He loveth and he desireth to love, for thus we know the love of God to stand; for the more we love, the more we yearn to love.

It is said, "They that eat me shall not hunger, and they that drink me, shall not thirst." Therefore the love of *Jesus* by itself is delectable and desirable. Therefore no joy shall be lacking for those that seek earnestly to love him whom angels desire to behold. Angels see him always, and ever desire to see him; for they are filled so full that their filling doth not take away their desire, and they desire so much that their desire doth not take away their fullness. This is full joy, this is glorious joy.

Therefore many men wish to joy with Christ, but as they love not his name, *Jesus*, they shall have sorrow without end, whatever they do. And if they give all things that they have to poor men, unless they love this name, *Jesus*, they shall labour in vain. For only such shall be gladdened in *Jesus* who have loved him in this present life. Those that defoul him with vices and foul thoughts, and turn not again, there is no doubt but they are put out from the glory of God. Therefore a man shall not see the glory of God, that hath not joyfully loved this name *Jesus*.

In truth, an evil man findeth not Jesus; for he sees him not where he is. He tries to seek *Jesus* in the joys of this world, where he shall never be found. Why therefore say ye idly, "We shall be saved in Jesus", while ye cease not to hate him, without whom ye cannot have health?

I am not surprised that a man, being tempted, falleth, if he does not have the name of *Jesus* lasting in his mind. Truly this name cleanses the conscience, makes the heart clear and clean, and drives away fear. It gets a man warmth of love and lifts up the mind to heavenly melody.

O thou good name! O thou sweet name! O glorious name! O healthful name! O name to be desired! Wicked spirits may not abide thee, when they behold Jesus, either in mind, or hear him named in mouth. I sought to love Jesus, and ever the more I grew complete in his love, so much the sweeter his name savoured to me. Therefore blessed be the name of Jesus for ever and ever, and so be it. Amen.

Sermon Four:
'Of The Love Of Jesus'

Unless a man be purified first by trials and sorrows, he may not come to the sweetness of God's love. O thou everlasting love, inflame my mind to love God, that it burn not except to his callings. O good Jesus! who else could give to me what I feel from thee. Thou must now be felt and not seen. Enter into the inmost recesses of my soul; come into mine heart and full fill it with thy most clear sweetness; make my mind to drink deeply of the strong wine of thy sweet love, that I, forgetting all evils, and all trivial thoughts, and disbelieving imaginations, may embrace thee only, joyfully rejoicing in my Lord Jesus.

Thou most sweet Lord, from henceforward leave me not, dwell with me in thy sweetness; for only thy presence is to me solace or comfort, and only thy absence leaves me sorrowful. O thou Holy Ghost, who inspirest where thou wilt, come into me, draw me to thee, that I may despise and set at nought in my heart all things of this world. Inflame my heart with thy love which shall forever burn upon thine altar. Come, I beseech thee, thou sweet and true joy; come thou sweetness so to be desired; come thou my beloved, who is all my comfort.

There are three degrees of Christ's love. Those who are chosen to God's love go from one to another. The first is called insuperable; the second is inseparable, the third is called singular.

Love is insuperable when it cannot be overcome with any other affection or love, no trial or temptation - when it gladly casts down all other hindrances, and all temptations, and quenches fleshly desires. When man suffers gladly and submissively all anguish for Christ, and is not overcome with any delight or flattering, so that whether thou art in ease or in anguish, in sickness or in health, that thou wouldest not, for all the world, anger God at any time. And blessed is the soul that is in this state; every labour is light to him that loveth truly, neither can any man better overcome labour than by love.

Love is inseparable when man's mind is inflamed with great love, and cleaves to Christ by inseparable thought; not allowing Christ to be any moment out of his mind, but as though he were bound in the heart, him he thinketh upon, and to him with great earnestness he draweth his spirit. Therefore, the love of Christ so groweth in the heart of the lover of God, and the despiser of the world, that it may not be overcome by any other affection or love. When man clingeth to Christ continuously, thinking upon him, forgetting him for no other occasion, then man's love is said to be inseparable and everlasting. And what love can be more or greater than this?

The third degree of love is singular. If thou seekest or receivest any other comfort than from thy God, even though thou lovest highly, thou lovest not singularly. This degree is highest and most wonderful to attain; for it hath no equal. Singular love is, when all warmth and comfort is closed out of the heart, except the love of Jesus alone. Other delight or other joy pleases not; for the sweetness of him is so comforting and lasting, his love is so burning and gladdening, that he who is in this degree may feel with joy the fire of love burning in his soul. That fire is so pleasant that no man can speak of it except he that feeleth it, and not fully he.

Then the soul is Jesus loving, on Jesus thinking, and Jesus desiring, burning in longing only for him; singing in him, resting on him. Then the thought turns to song and melody. The soul that is in this degree may boldly say, I mourn for love! I languish to come to my loved Jesus.

This degree of love cometh not of man's merit, but God giveth it freely, to whom he knoweth able to take it, and only where there is already great grace. Therefore, let no man presume more of himself than God hath called him to. But he that most withdraws his love from the world, and from unreasonable lusts, shall be most able, and most speedily increase in these degrees of love. Those that have liking in any other things than in Jesus, and in the sweetness of his law, come not to this degree of love.

In the first degree are some, in the second but few, in the third scarcely any. For the higher the living is, and the more it profits, the fewer lovers it hath; and the fewer followers.

The apostle Paul saith, "Some are like the light of the sun, some like the moon, and some like the stars." And so it is of the lovers of Jesus Christ. He that is in this degree of love, desireth to be unbound from the bond of his body, and to be in full joy with Jesus, whom he loveth. Therefore such a one in mourning for his long wait, may sing this song to his beloved Jesus, "When wilt thou come, my Beloved, to comfort me and bring me out of care, and give thyself to me, that I may see thee and dwell with thee for evermore? My Beloved, more than any other, when shall my heart break that I sorrow no more? Thy love hath wounded my heart, and I am desirous to depart, I stand still mourning for one lovely to love." His love draweth me. The bond of his love holdeth me away from worthless places and amusements, till I may get him – the sight of my Beloved who never shall go away.

Thus love moveth a soul in which it dwells, to sing of his Beloved, ever having the heart looking upward to the joys above. And this bringeth out love tears, languishing for joy. But these words are not pleasant to a fleshly soul. Love is a burning desire to God, with a wonderful delight in soul. Love uniteth the lover and the beloved. Love is the desire of the heart, ever thinking on that which it loveth. Love is a stirring of the soul to love God for himself, and all other things for God. This love putteth out all other love that is against God's will. Love is a right will, turned from all earthly things, and joined to God without departing, accompanied with the fire of the Holy Ghost.

Therefore take on love as the iron takes on the redness of fire, as air doth in the sun, as the wool in the dye. The coal heats the iron in the fire, so that it is all fire; the air is infused by the sun, so that it is all light; wool takes the hue, so that it changes all to the colour.

In this manner shall a lover of Jesus Christ do. He shall so burn in love that he shall be wholly turned into the fire of love; he shall so shine in virtues that no part of him be dark in vices.

Sermon Five:
'Of Meekness'

No soul can attain to any degree of true love to Jesus, unless he is truly meek. For a proud soul seeks to have his own will, and so shall he never come to any degree of God's love. The lower that a soul sitteth in the valley of meekness, the more streams of grace and love come to him. And if the soul be high in the hills of pride, the wind of the Fiend bloweth away from him all manner of goodness. Therefore as St Augustine biddeth, "Whoever wishes to attain to the bliss that is in heaven above, let him set the ground of his foundation here low in meekness." Nothing more overcometh the Fiend than meekness, and therefore he hateth it so much.

By two things principally, may a man know whether he is meek. If his heart be not moved, though his own will be contradicted and criticised – and when he is despised, falsely accused, and slandered; if his will stand unmoved, not desiring revenge, and his mouth be shut from unmeek answer. For he that hath entered truly into God's love, is not grieved, whatsoever slander, shame, or reproof he suffereth for the love of his Lord; but he is glad that he is worthy to suffer pain for Christ's love.

Wycliffe's memorial in Lutterworth church

Thus Christ's disciples went joying from the council of the Jews, that they were worthy to suffer despites and wrongs for the name of Jesus. For the apostle said, "All that will live meekly, and please Jesus Christ, shall suffer persecutions, and by many tribulations we must enter into the Kingdom of God. For it is given to such, not only that they believe in Christ, but also that they suffer for him." The prophet of God affirms, "Those that sought to do me evil spake vanities and thought deceit all day; but I as deaf heard not, and was as a dumb man not opening his mouth."

By seven tokens a man may suppose that he hath the love of Christ.

The first is, when all coveting of earthly things, and fleshly lusts, is weakened by him. For where coveting is, there is not the love of Christ. Then if a man have not coveting it is a sign that he hath love.

The second is, burning desire for heaven. For when he hath felt anything of it, the more he feeleth the more he wanteth, and he that hath felt nought, desireth nought.

The third token is, if his tongue be changed. That which used to speak of earth now speaketh of heaven.

The fourth is, exercise or practising what is for spiritual good. As when a man, leaving all other things, hath good will and devotion to prayer, and findeth sweetness therein.

The fifth is, when things which are hard in themselves, are made easy through love.

The sixth is, hardiness of soul to suffer all anguishes and troubles that befall. All the other tokens are not sufficient without this; for he that is righteous hateth nothing but sin; he loveth God alone; he hath no joy but in God; he feareth nothing except to offend God. And all his hope is to come to God.

The seventh is, joyfulness of soul when he is in tribulation, and that he love God, and thank him in all diseases that he suffers. It is the greatest token that he hath the love of God: when no woe, tribulation, or persecution, can bring him down from this love. Many love God, as they think, while they are in ease, but in adversity, or in sickness, they grudge against God, thinking that they do not deserve so to be punished for any sin they have done. And oftimes some say that God doeth them wrong. All such are feigned lovers, and have not the true love of God. For the Holy Ghost saith, "He that is a true friend loveth at all times."

Three principal advantages come from meekly suffering sickness. It cleanseth the soul from sin done before; it keepeth it from those into which it was likely to fall; it increaseth the reward in heaven, and gildeth the crown; and the longer it endureth the brighter becometh the crown. And in trust hereof St Paul said that he would joy gladly in his sicknesses, that the power of Christ dwell in him.

Sermon Six:
'Of Perfect Life'

Christ, not compelling, but freely counselling each man to perfect life, saith thus, "If any man will come after me let him deny himself, and take his cross and follow me" (Luke 9). Then let us forsake ourselves, that is, what we have made ourselves by sinning, and dwell as those who are changed by grace.

If a proud man be converted to Christ, and is made meek, he hath forsaken himself. If a covetous man ceaseth to covet, and giveth away his own things, he hath denied himself. If an evil liver changeth his life, he hath denied himself. The cross of Christ is taken up when compassion and pity towards our neighbour is truly kept; when man is crucified to the world, and the world crucified to him, setting the joy thereof at nought.

But let us not be so sure of the Lord's mercy, that we heap sins upon sins; neither say we while we are young, "Let us follow our desires, and in the end when old, repent from our sins, for the Lord is merciful, he shall not remember our sins." – Lord Jesus, turn us to thee, and then we shall be turned. Heal thou us, and we shall be truly whole. For without thy grace and help no man may be truly turned or healed. For they are but scorners who today turn to God, and tomorrow turn away.

What is turning to God? Nothing but turning from the world, from sin, and from the Fiend. What is turning from God? None but turning to the changeable goods of this world, to pleasing likeness of creatures, to works of the Fiend, and to lusts of the flesh. To be turned from the world, is to set at nought, and to put out of mind, all likings, joys, and mirths thereof, and to suffer meekly all bitterness, slanders, and troubles thereof, for the love of Christ; and to leave all occupations unlawful and unprofitable to the soul, so that man's will and thought be dead as far as seeking any thing that the world seeketh and loveth.

Therefore the prophet speaketh in the person of souls perfectly turning to God, saying, "Mine eyes," that is, my thought and intent, "shall ever be to God. For he shall draw my feet," that is, my soul and my affections, "out of the snare, and the net of the love of this world." He that is truly turned to God, fleeth from vices, beholdeth not the solaces or comforts of this world; but setteth his mind so stedfastly on God, that he well nigh forgetteth all outward things; he gathereth himself all within; he is lifted up wholly into Christ.

Those that will turn truly to Christ must flee occasions, words, sights, and deeds, tempting them to sin. For when the Fiend seeth one among a hundred who withstandeth his enticings, and turneth to God, and followeth the steps of Christ, by virtues, despising the joys of this present life, and seeking to love everlasting heavenly things, he findeth a thousand deceits to ensnare and trouble him, and a thousand manner of temptations to cast him down from God's love to the love of the world. And he beginneth with the smallest, that by foul thoughts he make him to be foul towards God.

He bringeth to man's mind the lusts which he had before, and suggesteth to him that he does not need to leave all his worldly and fleshly likings; and saith, It is too hard for a man to depart from all pleasure. He stirreth up fantasies, and vain thoughts innumerable, and unprofitable affections which before were asleep.

The Fiend reareth against such a soul, slanders, back bitings, persecutions, tribulations, false challenges, false accusings of various sins, and all manner of hatred. He calleth again to mind the delight he had in things he loved before. He enflameth the heart and the flesh with foul burnings. He beginneth by small enticings, and pursues to the greatest flame of wickedness. And he worketh thus busily to blow against us all manner of temptations and tribulations, because he seeth that by the mercy of God we are escaped out of his power. For he seeketh nothing so much as to separate a man from the holy and everlasting love of Jesus Christ, and to make him love failing things and uncleanness of this world.

Sermon Seven: 'Of Temptation'

He that is truly fed with the bread that came down from heaven, boweth not his love to those things to which the Fiend enticeth. Temptations are overcome by patience and meek suffering. What is patience? – a glad and willing suffering of troubles. He that is patient, murmurs not at adversity, but rather, at all times, praises God.

Evil men always grudge in adversities, and flee from them as much as they may. For as long as they are totally given to material things, they are deprived of true hope of everlasting things. They find solace or comfort only in earthly goods, for they have lost the taste for heavenly things.

There is no soul of man in this world which clingeth not either to the Creator or the things created. If he love the created he loseth God, and goeth to death with that which he loveth. Such love in the beginning is hard labour and folly, in the middle it is languor and wretchedness, and in the end it is hate and pain.

He that truly loveth his Maker, refuseth to desire any things that are in the world. It is sweetness for him to speak of him and be with him; to think upon his Maker is refreshing to him. He closes his outer senses lest death enter in by the windows, lest he be occupied unprofitably with any vanity. Sometimes there are reared against him despisings, reproofs, scorns, and slanders. Therefore it is needful that he take the shield of patience, and be ready to forget and to forgive all wrongs, and to pray for the turning to good of them that hate him and hurt him.

No man knows his true self whether he be strong or feeble, unless he is tempted when he is at peace. Many men seem to be patient when they are not in trouble, but when a light blast, not of injustice, but of correction, touches them, their mind quickly turns into bitterness and wrath, and if they hear one word said against their will, they reply with two stronger ones. Into their council come not, O my soul!

The darts of the enemy are to be quenched with the meekness and sweetness of the love of Christ. Do not give way to temptation, be it ever so grievous. For the greater the battle the more glorious the victory, and the higher the crown. Blessed is the man that suffereth temptation, for when he is proved to be true, he shall take a crown of life. Flee as much as thou canst from the praising of men. Despise favour, worship, and all vain glory, and gladly sustain or suffer enmities, hates, backbitings, or reproofs. And so by a bad name, and by good praise; by tribulations and gladnesses, cease thou not to press forward to heavenly kingdoms.

When thou art tempted or troubled, think upon the remedy that our Saviour saith in his gospel: "Watch ye and pray ye, that ye enter not into temptation." He saith not, "Pray ye that ye be not tempted." For it is good and profitable for good men to be tempted and troubled, as is shown by what the prophet saith, "To him that is tempted and troubled, God saith, I am with him in tribulation; I shall deliver him, and shall glorify him."

Let no man think himself to be holy because he is not tempted, for the holiest and highest in life have the most temptations. The higher a hill is, the greater is the wind at the top; so, the higher the life is, so the stronger is the temptation of the enemy.

God playeth with his child when he allows him to be tempted, as a mother rises from her much beloved child, and hides herself, and leaves him alone, and allows him to cry, Mother, Mother, so that he looks about, cries and weeps for a time, and at last when the child is ready to be overset with troubles and weeping, she comes again, clasps him in her arms, and kisses him, and wipes away the tears. So our Lord alloweth his beloved child to be tempted and troubled for a time, and withdraweth some of his solace and full protection, to see what his child will do; and when he is about to be overcome by temptations, then he defendeth him, and comforteth him with his grace. And therefore, when we are tempted, let us cry for the help of our Father, as a child cries after the comfort of its mother. For whoso prayeth devoutly, shall have help oft to pray. Devout prayer of a holy soul, is as sweet incense which driveth away all evil savours, and enters up as an odour of sweetness into the presence of God.

Sermon Eight:
'The Charter Of Our Heavenly Heritage'

Every wise man that claims his heritage, asks great pardon, keeps busy, and oft has his mind upon the charter of that which he claims. Therefore, let each man learn to live virtuously, and keep his mind upon the charter of heaven's bliss, and study stedfastly the meaning of this decree, for the pardon thereof shall endure without end.

Understand well that the charter of this heritage, and the infallible decree of this everlasting pardon, is our *Lord Jesus Christ*, written with all the might and goodness of God.

The parchment of this heavenly charter is neither of sheep skin nor of calf, but it is of the body of our Lord Jesus, a lamb that never was spotted with spot of sin. And there never was skin of sheep or of calf so sorely and so hard strained upon the tools of any parchment maker, as the blessed body of our Lord Jesus Christ, which for our love, was strained and drawn upon the cross.

No man ever heard from the beginning of the world until now, nor shall hear from hence to doomsday, that a writer ever wrote upon sheep skin or upon calf skin, with such hard and hideous pens, so bitterly, so sorely, and so deeply, as the accursed Jews wrote upon the blessed body of our Lord Jesus Christ, with hard nails, sharp spear, and sore pricking thorns, instead of their pens. They wrote so sorely and so deep, that they pierced his hands and feet with hard nails. They opened his heart with a sharp spear. They pressed upon his head a crown of sharp thorns. The wounds upon that blessed body are the letters with which our charter was written, by which we may claim our heritage, if we live rightly, and keep the charter stedfastly in mind.

The subject of the words written within and without this blessed charter, and body of Jesus Christ, is our belief. For he is the strongbox in whom is inclosed and locked all this treasure of knowledge, and wisdom of God.

Upon this blessed charter was written wailing, or mourning, and sorrow. Wailing or mourning for sorrow of our sins – which in order to be healed and washed away, Christ, God and man, must suffer such hard and painful wounds. Upon Christ's body, that is our heavenly charter, was written joy and singing, to all those that completely forsake their sins. For they have full medicine and help, by virtue of the bitter wounds and precious blood of Jesus. And upon the wounds of Jesus, may be read sorrow for all them that for wrong desire and lust which endureth but a while, bind themselves to sin and serving the Fiend, and lose the help of the heavenly charter, and so lose their heritage, and go blindly to sorrow that endureth for ever.

The laces [the strings by which the seal is attached] of this heavenly charter are the promises of God; and those of a God who may not lie, for he is sovereign truth.

The first, is his promise, that whatever day or hour a sinful man or woman leave their sin, wholly, and heartily, with bitter sorrow, and turn to him, he shall receive them in his mercy. But let each man beware that he tarry not too long, lest for his carelessness grace be taken from him.

The second, is the full trust we have that God may not lie, neither be false in his promise. And herein depends surely our trust of our heritage. By these two hang the seal of our charter, sealed with the blood of the Lamb, even Christ.

The print of this seal is the form of our Lord Jesus hanging for our sin on the cross. He hath his head bowed down, ready to kiss all those that truly turn to him. He hath his arms spread abroad, ready to embrace them. He is nailed fast, hand and foot, to the cross, for he will dwell with them, and never go away from man, but man forsook him first through sin. He hath all his body spread out to give himself wholly to us, and he hath his side opened, and his heart cloven for our sake, so that without hindrance we may creep into Christ's heart, and rest there by stedfast belief and hearty love.

This charter no fire can burn, nor water drown, nor thief rob, nor any creature destroy. For this scripture the Father of heaven hath made secure, and sent it into the world, scripture which may not be undone, as the gospel witnesses. This scripture is our **Lord Jesus Christ**, the charter of our heritage of heaven.

Lock not this charter in thy strongbox but put it, or write it in thine heart, and none of the creatures, either in heaven, or on earth, or in hell, can steal it, or tear it from thee; but if thou govern thyself from assenting to sin, and keepest well this charter in the strongbox of thine heart with good living and devout love, all thy days – as surely and truly as he is the true God, by virtue of this charter, thou shalt have thine heritage of bliss, enduring without end.

Therefore, may we hasten to repentance, as Augustine bids, and let the last day be often before our eyes. Refrain we our bodies from vices and evil covetings, and ever let our heart think heavenly things, that when we shall arrive there we may fully use heavenly goods. For why? We believe that when our soul shall be unknit from the bond of flesh, if we have lived well and rightly before God, the companies of angels shall bring us to worship the true Doomsman [Judge].

If we live, as I said, and do those things that are pleasing to God, then peace shall be our compass [a circle around us] and security. Then we shall not dread the fiery darts of the devil, nor any manner of enemy that desires to hurt our souls. The flesh shall no more be adversary to the spirit, nor shall we dread any perils. Then the Holy Ghost shall give to us a dwelling in heavenly things, and we, glad and joyful, shall await the day of doom to come, in which the souls of all men shall receive reward for their deeds. Then sinners and unpiteous men shall perish. And when all these shall deserve to be sentenced to the fire of hell for their sins and their great trespasses, so then, if we have pleased God while we were here in body, we shall have everlasting reward with saints.

Therefore let us despise all things that are vain and failing, that we may receive great glory from Christ. Therefore turn we away from vices and go we to virtues, nor let superfluous words come out of our mouths, for we shall give account for idle words in the day of doom.

Therefore, use thou the fellowship of godly men, and turn not away thine ears from their words. For the words of men that fear God, are words of life and holiness of soul to them that hear and understand them. As the sun rising, driveth away the mist, so the teaching of holy men casteth away the darkness from our hearts.

I beseech you, shun proud men, envious men, backbiters, liars, swearers, and men despising their salvation, who are dead to virtues, and joy in their own lusts, and lack God's joy. I speak not only of those that are in thy house, but wherever thou shalt hear such, shun them, and come thou not with such men if thou canst not dissuade them from their error. For by one sickly sheep all the flock is defiled, and a little portion of gall turns much sweetness into bitterness. For though a man seem to thee clean in clothing, and noble in bringing forth sweet words, nevertheless if he doeth the contrary works, his hypocrisy hurts more than his figure or his words can please.

And every work that thou thinkest to do, first think thou in God, and examine diligently whether the work is of God; and if it be rightful before God, perform it, or else cut it away from thy soul. And likewise be aware of each wickedness and sin, in word and deed, in thought, in hands, in feet, in sight, and in hearing, and keep we our body and our soul.

For Jesus Christ our Lord God, the Son of God the Father, that came down from heaven to earth, he was lifted up on the cross, and died for us sinners, to deliver us from the tormenting of the devil. He suffered pain to deliver us from everlasting pain. He suffered death to deliver us from death. He rose again from death, that we should rise again in body and soul in the last day of the great doom. And therefore it is said of the first church, that one heart, one will, and one soul was in them for the Lord.

Lord, give me grace to hold righteousness in all things; spiritual hardiness and temperance, that I may lead a clean and blessed life, and prudently flee evil, and that I may understand the treacherous and deceitful falseness of the devil, lest he beguile me under the pretence of goodness. Make me mild, well-willing, peaceable, courteous, and temperate, and to accord goodness without feigning, unto all. And make me stedfast and strong.

And also, Lord, give thou to me, to act in mildness, that I be quiet in words, that I speak what is appropriate and that I speak not that which it is not right to speak. Give me grace to keep the faith unspotted without any errors, and that my works henceforth be worthy.

Sermon Nine: 'On Prayer'

Our Lord Jesus Christ teacheth us to pray continually for all needful things, both for our body and our soul; for in the gospel of St Luke Christ saith it is needful to pray continually and St Paul bids christian men pray without ceasing or hindrance. For St James saith, that the fervent and lasting prayer of a just man is of much worth.

And while Moses was in the mount, and held up his hands, and prayed for his people, his people had victory over their enemies; and when he ceased to pray thus, his people were overcome, as the second book of Holy Writ teaches. So if priests dwell in the mount of high spiritual life, and espy deceits of the devil, and show them to the people by true preaching, and hold up their hands, that is open good works, and continue in them; and pray with fervent desire to perform righteousness of God's law and command – then christian people shall have victory over the devil and cursed sin, then shall rest and peace, and love dwell among them. And if priests cease this holy life and good example, and this desire of righteousness, then christian people shall be much overcome by sin, and have pestilence and wars, and woe enough; and unless God help, more endless woe in hell.

King Hezekiah, by holy prayer and weeping and sorrow, got forgiveness for his sin, and fifteen years of his life; and the sun went back, ten degrees on the dial, as Isaiah's book witnesses. Also by the prayer of the holy leader Joshua, the sun and moon stood still all day, to give light to pursue God's enemies, who desired to quench God's name, his law, and his people.

Therefore Christ saith to his disciples, "If ye ask my Father any thing in my name, he shall give it to you"; but we ask in the name of Jesus, when we ask any thing needful or profitable for the saving of men's souls, so we should ask this devoutly, with great desire, and wisely, humbly and perseveringly by firm faith, true hope, and lasting love; and whatever we ask thus, we shall have of the Father of heaven.

Also Christ saith thus in the gospel, "evil men have wisdom. If ye give good things to your children, how much more shall your Father, of heaven, give a good Spirit to men that ask him." Then, since nature teaches sinful men to give goods to their children, how much more will God, author of goodness and love, give spiritual goods, profitable to the soul, to his children whom he loves so much! Therefore ask of God heavenly things, such as grace, will, wisdom, and power to serve God, to please him; and not for worldly goods, except as much as is needful to sustain thy life in truth and service of thy God.

See now how wicked men's prayers displease God, and harm themselves and the people. God himself speaks in this way to evil men that pray to him in need: "I have called, and ye have forsaken and have despised all my blamings, and I shall despise your perishing, and shall scorn you. When that which ye have dreaded shall come to you, then ye shall call and I shall not hear, for they hated discipline.

They retained not the fear of the Lord, and they assented not to my counsel."

And by the prophet Isaiah, God saith thus to wicked men: "Ye princes of Sodom, hear the Lord's word; people of Gomorrah, understand with thine ears the law of our Lord God. Your incense is abomination to me. I shall not suffer your new moon, which is a principal feast and sabbath, and other feasts. Your companies are evil, my soul hath hated your feasts of months, and solemnities. They are made to me heavy and troublous, and when ye shall hold forth your hands I will turn mine eyes away from you. And when ye shall make many prayers I will not hear, for your hands are full of blood." that is of wrong, slaying of men, and foul sins.

Also, God saith that the prayer of the man who turneth away his ear that he hear not the law, is abominable and cursed. Therefore David saith, "If I have beholden wickedness in my heart, the Lord shall not hear by grace." that is, if I wilfully and gladly do wickedness. God saith to the sinful man: "Why talkest thou about my righteousness, and takest my testament in thy mouth?" And the Holy Ghost saith of Judas Iscariot, "His prayer was made into sin." and our Lord Jesus saith, "This people worship me with lips, but their heart is far from me, but they teach learning and commandments of men, worshipping me without cause." - that is such men as teach and enforce men's laws and traditions and

Monument at Lutterworth

ye to me, Lord, Lord, and do not the things that I commanded?" for Jesus saith: "Woe to you scribes and pharisees, hypocrites, that devour widows' houses, praying long prayers, therefore ye shall receive greater judgment." Truly it is written, "the sacrifices of wicked men are abominable to the Lord, the vows of sacrifices of just men are pleasant." For in the day of doom of God Almighty he will not want to know what is given, but who gave it. Therefore it is written in Holy Writ: "The Lord had respect for Abel and his gifts."

The mighty God approveth not the gifts of wicked men, nor looketh on their offerings, nor shall have mercy on sinners for the multitude of their sacrifices.

What a wonder it is that men praise God so much by this new praying: by great crying and high song, and leave the still manner of praying as Christ and his apostles did. It seems that we seek our own pleasure and pride in the song, more than the devotion and understanding of what we sing. This is great sin, for Augustine saith: "As oft as the song delights me more than that which is sung, so oft I acknowledge that I trespass grievously."

Shall this new song excuse us from learning and preaching the gospel that Christ taught and commanded? Therefore ye that are priests live well, pray devoutly, and teach the gospel truly and freely, as Christ and his apostles did. Amen.

commandments, more than Holy Writ and God's commandments, vainly and falsely worship God.

Also Jesus saith to wicked men, "Why say

Sermon Ten:
'Twelve Hindrances to Prayer'

Here follow twelve hindrances to prayer, whereby men may know better why they are not always heard when they pray to God.

The first hindrance to prayer, is the sin of him that prayeth. In Isaiah 59: "Your wickednesses have separated you from your God; and your sins have hidden his face from you, so that he will not hear." And in Jeremiah 5: "Our sins have kept God from us." And in Lamentations 3: "We have done wickedly, and have deserved vengeance; therefore thou mayest not be prayed, [that is, pleased by our prayer]. And oft thou hast covered thyself with a cloud, that a prayer pass not through." And David saith in the Psalter: "If I beheld wickedness in my heart," [that is to say, If I loved wickedness], "God shall not hear."

The second hindrance is, the doubt of him that prayeth. In James 1 it is said: "Let a man ask in faith, nothing doubting, for he that doubteth is like a wave of the sea, which is driven of the wind, and tossed about. Let not that man guess that he shall get any thing of the Lord." And Bernard saith: "He is proved unworthy to have heavenly blessings, that asketh of God with doubting desire."

The third hindrance is this, that a man asketh not that which ought to be asked. In Matthew 20 it is said: "Ye know not what ye ask." Oft the church is not heard, when it asketh that tribulations be taken away.

The fourth hindrance is, being unworthy of him to whom we pray. For God, in Jeremiah 7 & 11 saith: "Pray not thou for this people, for I shall not hear thee." And in Jeremiah 15 God saith thus: "Though Moses and Samuel stand before me, my will is not to this people; cast them out from my face and go they out."

The fifth hindrance is, the multitude of evil thoughts. In Genesis 15, Abraham drove away the birds; that is, he that prayeth shall drive away evil thoughts.

The sixth hindrance is, the despising of God's law. In Proverbs 28 God saith: "The prayer of him that turneth away his ear, that he hear not the law of God, shall be abominable, or cursed." And in Proverbs 1 "They shall call me to help", saith God, "and I shall not hear them; for they hated teaching and chastising."

The seventh hindrance is, hardness of soul; and this is of two types. Some is hardness against poor men, of which it is said in Proverbs 21: "If a man stoppeth his ear at the cry of a poor man, he shall cry and he shall not be heard." Another hardness is to them that have trespassed, when a man will not forgive them. In Mark 11 Christ saith: "When ye stand to pray, forgive ye, if ye have any thing against any man; that also your Father which is in heaven, forgive to you your sins. That if ye forgive not men, neither shall your Father forgive you your sins."

The eighth hindrance is, increase of sin. In James 4 he saith: "Draw nigh to God, and he shall draw nigh to you." He draweth nigh to God, that ceaseth from evil work. Concerning this hindrance, and that which goeth before, Isidore speaks, and saith thus, "In two manners a prayer is hindered, that a man may not get the things that are asked; one is, if a man do yet evils, that is, wilfully continueth in sin; and the other is, if he forgive not sin to man that trespasseth against him."

The ninth hindrance is, suggestions of the Devil; that keep many men from prayer.

The tenth hindrance is, littleness of desire. Augustine saith, "God keepeth that thing from thee, which he will not give soon to thee, that thou learn to desire great things."

The eleventh hindrance is, the impatience of him that asketh. In 1 Samuel 28 Saul asked counsel of the Lord, and he answered not Saul. And Saul said: "Seek ye for me a woman that hath an evil spirit."

The twelfth hindrance is, the lack of perseverance in prayer. In Luke 11 Christ saith: "If a man continueth knocking at the gate, the friend [that is, God] shall rise and give him as many loaves as he needeth."

Now hast thou here twelve hindrances to prayer, well grounded in Holy Scripture. It is good, before thou prayest, to search thy conscience, so that thy prayer is not hindered by any of these, and so by grace to have the answer to thy prayer, and eventually to come to bliss without end.

Sermon Eleven: 'A Short Rule of Life'

First, when thou risest, or fully wakest, think upon the goodness of thy God; how because of his own goodness, and not for any need, he made all things out of nothing, both angels and men, and all other creatures.

The second time, think on the great sufferings, and willing death that Christ suffered for mankind. When no man might make payment for the guilt of Adam and Eve, and many others, neither could any angel make payment, then Christ from his endless love, suffered such great passion and painful death, that no creature could suffer so much.

Think the third time, how God hath saved thee from death and other mischief, and suffered many thousands to be lost the previous night, some in water, and some in fire, and some by sudden death; and some to be damned without end. And for this goodness and mercy thank thy God with all thine heart. And pray him to give thee grace to spend in that day, and evermore, all the powers of thy soul, thy mind, understanding, reason, and will; and all the powers of thy body, thy strength, beauty, and thy five senses, in his service and worship, and in doing nothing against his commandments; but in willing performance of his works of mercy, and in giving a good example of holy life, both in word and deed to all men about thee.

Next, be sure that thou art well occupied, and no time idle, because of the danger of temptation. Take meat and drink in moderation, not too costly, and be not too particular about them. But such as God sendeth thee with health, take it in such amounts that thou be fresher in mind and understanding to serve God. And always thank him for such gifts.

Besides this, be sure that thou do right and fairly to all men, thy superiors, equals, and subjects or servants; and stir them all to love truth, and mercy, and true peace, and love.

Also, most of all fear God and his wrath; and most of all love God and his law, and his worship; and ask not principally for worldly reward, but in all thine heart desire the bliss of heaven, in the mercy of God, and a holy life; and think much of the dreadful doom of pains of hell, in order to keep thee out of sin; and on the endless great joys of heaven, in order to keep thee in virtuous life; and according to thy skill teach others to do the same.

At the end of the day think where thou hast offended God, and how much and how oft, and therefore have entire sorrow, and amend it while thou mayest. And think how many God hath allowed to perish that day, in many ways, and to be damned everlastingly, and how graciously he hath saved thee; not for thy deserving, but for his own mercy and goodness, and therefore thank him with all thine heart. And pray to him for grace that thou mayest dwell and end in his true and holy service and real love, and teach other men to do the same.

If thou art a ***priest*** and especially one having the charge of souls, live thou holily, surpassing other men in holy prayer, desire, and thinking, in holy speaking, counselling, and true teaching.

And may God's commands, his gospel, and virtues, be ever in thy mouth; and ever despise sin, and seek to draw men from it; and may thy deeds be so rightful that no man shall blame them with reason, but may thy open deeds be a true book to all thy people and unlearned men, to serve God and do his commands thereby. For an example of good a life, open and lasting, stirreth men more than true preaching by word only.

And waste not thy goods in great feasts of rich men, but live a humble life, of poor men's alms and goods, both in meat, and drink, and clothes, and the remainder give truly to poor men that have not of their own, and may not labour for feebleness or sickness, and thus thou shalt be a true priest both to God and man.

If thou art a ***lord*** [or master, one having authority over others], ensure that thou live a rightful life in thine own person, both in respect to God and man, keeping the commands of God, doing the works of mercy, ruling well thy five senses, and doing reason, and equity, and good conscience to all men.

In the second place, govern well thy wife, thy children, and thy household attendants, in God's law, and allow no sin among them, neither in word nor in deed, that they may be examples of holiness and righteousness to all others, for thou shalt be condemned for their evil life and their evil example, unless thou amend it as much as thou art able.

In the third place, govern well thy tenants, and maintain them in right and reason, and be merciful to them in their rents. And chastise in good manner them that are rebels against God's commands and virtuous life, more than for rebellion against thine own cause; otherwise thou lovest more thine own cause than God's, and thyself more than God Almighty, thou wert then a false traitor to God. And love, reward, praise, and cherish the true and virtuous of life more than if thou sought only thine own profit.

And reverence and maintain truly, according to thy skill and might, God's law and true preachers of it, and God's servants, in rest and peace. Thou doest wrong against God, if thou maintainest antichrist's disciples in their errors against Christ's life and his teaching, and helpest to slander and pursue true men that teach Christ's gospel and his life.

If thou art a **labourer**, live in meekness, and truly and willingly do thy labour, that thy lord or thy master if he be a heathen man, by thy meekness, willing and true service, may not have to grudge against thee, nor slander thy God, nor thy christian profession; but rather be stirred to come to christianity.

And serve not christian lords with grudgings; not only in their presence, but truly and willingly, and in absence. Not only for worldly dread, or worldly reward, but for dread of God and conscience, and for reward in heaven. For God that putteth thee in such service knoweth what state is best for thee, and will reward thee more than all earthly lords may, if thou dost it truly and willingly obeying him.

And in all things beware of grudging against God and the trials sent by him: in great labour, long or great sickness, and other adversities. And beware of wrath, of cursing, of speaking evil of man or beast; and ever keep patience, meekness, and love, both to God and man.

And thus each man in the three states ought to live, to save himself, and to help others; and thus should good life, rest, peace, and love, be among christian men, and they be saved, and heathen men soon converted, and God magnified greatly.

Sermon Twelve:
'Antichrist's Labour to Destroy Holy Writ'

As our Lord Jesus Christ ordained that the writing of the four evangelists, would make his gospel surely known, and maintained against heretics, and men out of the faith; so the devil, even Satan, devises by antichrist and his worldly false priests, to destroy Holy Writ and christian men's belief, by four accursed ways, or false reasons: (1) The church is of more authority, and more to be believed than any gospel. (2) That Augustine said he would not believe the gospel if the church had not taught him to. (3) That no man alive knows which is the gospel, but by the approving of the church. (4) If men say that they believe this is the gospel of Matthew or John, they ask: "Why believest thou that this is the gospel?"

These four arguments, and many more, the Fiend makes, to blind men in their belief, that they should not know what is sin, or what is virtue; which is truth, which is falsehood; which is good, which is evil; which are God's commands, and which are the Fiend's lies; thus to bring all men blindly to hell and their new religion.

And principally friars preach these arguments and sow them among ignorant men in the country, to stop poor priests and ignorant men from speaking the gospel, Holy Writ, God's commandments, joys of heaven, of sin, and of the pains of hell, lest they stir men to rise out of their sins for dread of pains, and to live in virtuous life, to have the bliss of heaven. And this error in belief is made and committed by these accursed pharisees to magnify their new feigned orders, founded by sinful men, not with Christ's holy religion.

1). Let us now discuss the first evil argument, that the church of more authority and credence than the gospel. They say that Nicodemus and many others wrote Gospels of Christ's life, and his teaching; but the church rejected them and approved the four gospels of Matthew, Mark, Luke, and John; since it was in full power of the church to reject and condemn which they would, and to approve and to accept, which they liked, and therefore, they say, men should believe the church more than any gospel.

These crafty heretics understand by the church: the pope of Rome and his cardinals, and the multitude of worldly priests assenting to his worldly lordship, above all kings and emperors of this world.

True men say that the clergy who originally were wise, and holy of life, were stirred up by the Holy Ghost, to take these four gospels. And these four witnesses were accepted of the Holy Ghost, to write these things for man's instruction. But the church could not possibly have rejected the gospels, and accepted others; for then it would have gone against the will of God.

These men wish to make their life and teachings to be the gospel and belief of christian men; but who are greater traitors to God and his law, and more perilous and false prophets to christian people, than these men? For God commandeth, on pain of his great curse and deep condemnation, that no man remove any point of truth from his law, nor add to it any new thing that is not approved by the Trinity. And Jesus Christ saith, that his gospel is an everlasting testament; but they will undo it with the vile breath of antichrist's mouth.

2). See now the second wheel in this devil's wagon. They quote Augustine that he saith thus: That he would not believe the gospel unless the church said he should.

True men being told this, suppose that Augustine said this word. But he said it with this meaning: That unless Christ said and approved this gospel, he would not believe it; but they interpret it that unless the multitude of accursed worldly priests accept that it is the gospel, Augustine would not believe the gospel of Jesus Christ; and since Augustine was and is so great a doctor of holy church, no man should believe the gospel, unless these prelates confirm that this is the gospel of Christ.

Men must under threat of damnation, receive their wicked teachings as belief, and forsake the gospel of Christ, and take Fiend's lies instead of God's lore! And more cursedness to destroy christian men's faith, come from this falsehood, than man or fiend, can imagine till the day of doom.

Therefore, Christians should stand to the death for maintaining Christ's gospel and true understanding thereof, gotten by holy life and great study, and not set their faith or trust in sinful prelates and their priests, nor in their understanding of Holy Writ. For Christ saith in the gospel, that the Father of heaven hideth these truths from worldly wise men, and conceited, and showeth them to meek men, as were Christ's disciples.

3). See now the third wheel of Satan's car; these deceitful priests and religious men of Lucifer say, that no man knows which is the gospel, except by the approving and confirming of the church.

But true men say that this is full of falsehood. For christian men are certain of their belief, that this truth, taught by Christ and his apostles, is the gospel, though all antichrist's priests cry ever so certain to the contrary, with the threat of curse, imprisonment, and burning. And this belief is not grounded on the pope and his cardinals, for then it must fail and be undone, as they fail and some time are destroyed; but it is grounded on Jesus Christ, God and man, and on the Holy Trinity. Jesus Christ is our God and our best Master ever ready to teach true men all things that are profitable, and needful to their souls.

4). The fourth wheel of Belial's cart is this; when christian men say they know by belief that this is Christ's gospel, these malicious heretics ask, "Why do they believe that this is gospel?"

But true men reply, "Why do they believe that God is God?" But these heretics claim that whatever the prelates teach openly, and maintain stedfastly, has as great authority or more than Christ's gospel. But christian men take their faith from God, by his gracious gift, when he giveth it to them; so that they might know and understand truths needful to save men's souls, and by grace believe in their hearts such truths. This men call faith, and because of this faith, christian men are more certain than any man is of worldly things, by any bodily knowledge.

Therefore, Christ reproved most the lack of belief, both in the Jews, and in his disciples; and therefore, Christ's apostles prayed most to have stableness in faith, for it is impossible that any man please God without faith; and so Christ prayed principally that the faith of Peter and other disciples should not fail.

And God's law tells how by faith saints wrought all their great wonders and marvels that they did; and if antichrist say here, that each man may pretend that he hath right faith, and a good understanding of Holy Writ given of God, when he is in error, let a man seek in all things truly the honour of God, and live justly to God and man, and God will not fail to give him any thing that is needful to him, neither in faith, nor understanding, nor in answer against his enemies. And faith is the shield of christian men against all temptations of the Fiend, and the ground of all virtues.

Christian men should know how the new religionists [the friars] are false prophets and accursed sects, of which Christ and his apostles prophesied before. John the evangelist commandeth that christian men should not receive them into their houses, nor greet them.

May God almighty strengthen his little flock against these four wheels of Satan's car, against antichrist's priests and helpers, and make them strong in righteous faith, hope, and love, to seek truly the worship of Jesus Christ, and the saving of men's souls, to despise antichrist's boast and pretended power, and willingly and joyfully to suffer pain and reproof in the world, for the name of Jesus and his gospel, to give firm a example to others, to follow and reach the high bliss of heaven by glorious martyrdom as other saints did before.

May Jesus of his endless might, endless wisdom, endless goodness, and love, grant to us sinful wretches this favour. Amen.

Bibliography

Workman: *'John Wycliffe'* (2 volumes).
Vaughan: *'Life of Wycliffe'* (2 volumes).
Lechler: *'John Wycliffe and his English Precursors'*.
Trevelyan: *'England in the Age of Wycliffe'*.
Trevelyan: *'English Social History'*.
Stacey: *'Wycliffe and Reform'*.
Hague: *'John Wycliffe'*.
MacFarlane: *'John Wycliffe and English Nonconformity'*.
Thompson: *'The Later Lollards'*.
Dickens: *'Lollards and Protestants in the Diocese of York, 1509-1558'*.
Wylie: *'History of Protestantism'*.
Webb le Bas: *'Life of Wycliffe'*.
Burrows: *'Wycliffe's Place in History'*.
d'Aubigne: *'Reformation in England'*.
Parker: *'The Morning Star'*.
Sergeant: *'John Wycliffe'*.
John F. Davis: *'Heresy and Reformation in the South East of England 1520-1559'*
(Royal Historical Society Monograph)
'Writings of John Wycliffe' – the Religious Tract Society.
'Tracts and Treaties of John Wycliffe' – the Wycliffe Society.
Revd John Lewis: *'Brief History of the English Anabaptists'*
(Bodleian Library M.S. Rawlinson c409 p26)